W9-ACA-294

# WOMAN IN MIND

By the Same Author

A CHORUS OF DISAPPROVAL

# *WOMAN IN MIND*

## December Bee

## ALAN AYCKBOURN

First published in 1986 by Faber and Faber Limited, 3 Queen Square
London WC1N 3AU

Filmset by Wilmaset Birkenhead Wirral
Printed in Great Britain by Redwood Burn Limited Trowbridge Wilt-
shire

# CHARACTERS

SUSAN

BILL, her doctor
GERALD, her husband
MURIEL, her sister-in-law
RICK, her son

ANDY, her husband
TONY, her brother
LUCY, her daughter

The action occurs within forty-eight hours and takes place in Susan's garden and beyond.

*Woman in Mind* was first performed in Scarborough at the Stephen Joseph Theatre in the Round on 30 May 1985. The cast was as follows:

| | |
|---|---|
| SUSAN | Ursula Jones |
| BILL | Barry McCarthy |
| ANDY | Robin Herford |
| TONY | John Hudson |
| LUCY | Caroline Webster |
| GERALD | Russell Dixon |
| MURIEL | Heather Stoney |
| RICK | Tom Bowles |
| | |
| *Director* | Alan Ayckbourn |
| *Designer* | Adrian P. Smith |

The New York premiere of *Woman in Mind* was presented by the Manhattan Theatre Club at City Center on February 17, 1988. The cast was as follows:

| | |
|---|---|
| SUSAN | Stockard Channing |
| BILL | Simon Jones |
| ANDY | Daniel Gerroll |
| TONY | Michael Countryman |
| LUCY | Tracy Pollan |
| GERALD | Remak Ramsay |
| MURIEL | Patricia Conolly |
| RICK | John David Cullum |
| | |
| *Directed* | Lynne Meadow |
| *Sets* | John Lee Beatty |
| *Costumes* | Ann Roth |
| *Lighting* | Pat Collins |

# ACT ONE

ACT ONE

*Darkness.*

*We hear the sound of a woman moaning as she regains conscious-
ness. As she opens her eyes, there is bright, afternoon garden sunlight.
Throughout the play, we will hear what she hears; see what she sees.
A subjective viewpoint therefore and one that may at times be somewhat less than accurate.*

*The woman is* SUSAN. *She is lying on the grass in the middle of her
small, tidy, suburban garden.*

SUSAN:  Aaaah!

(BILL WINDSOR, *a pleasant, rather nervous GP is kneeling on the
grass a little away from her, attempting to open his medical case
without much success. He fails to see her for a minute, so engrossed
is he in his abortive task.* SUSAN *watches him. She is an unassum-
ing woman in her forties, used to and happy to play second fiddle
to more determinedly motivated personalities than her own. Only
now, at this stage of her life, is she beginning to question this role
she's played or perhaps been cast in.* BILL *is a year or two younger,
eager to reassure, quick to apologize for his own shortcomings. Not
though, alas, an instinctive healer of the sick. He notices* SUSAN *is
awake.)*

BILL:  Ah! Score ache . . .

SUSAN:  *(Trying to sit up)* Waah . . .

BILL:  Wo! Won't spider slit up pikelet . . .

SUSAN:  What?

BILL:  Skater baby.

SUSAN:  *(Trying again to sit up, alarmed)* What are you saying—*(Clasping her head)*—Ah!

BILL:  *(Pushing her back, gently)* Squeezy . . . squeezy . . .

SUSAN:  Squeezy?

BILL:  Score grounds appeal cumquat doggy Martha hat sick on the bed . . .

SUSAN:  Sick on the what?

BILL:  Squeezy, cow, squeezy . . .

SUSAN:  I've no idea what you're saying. What are you saying?

BILL:  Saul bite. Saul bite.

SUSAN:  Who are you, anyway? Where am I?

BILL:  Octer bin sir. Climb octer bin sir. Mrs sure pardon choose 'un.

SUSAN:  Oh, God, I've died. That's what it is. I've died. And—wherever it is I've gone—nobody speaks English . . . What am I going to do? What am I going to do?

BILL:  Choose 'un, choose 'un. Pea squeak jinglish. Pie squeaking jinglish cow. Choose 'un . . .

SUSAN: *(Tearful now)* I'm in hell. I've died and gone to hell.

BILL: Choose 'un . . .

SUSAN: Why have I gone to hell? Why me? I've tried so terribly hard, too. Terribly hard . . .

BILL: Susan . . .

SUSAN: You've no idea how hard I've tried. There must be some mistake . . .

BILL: Susan . . . ?

SUSAN: Susan? Yes, that's me. Susan. *(Pointing at herself, loudly, as to a foreigner)* Me Susan, yes.

BILL: You're Susan, yes.

SUSAN: Susan, yes. Thank heavens.

BILL: December bee?

SUSAN: December bee? Oh, dear God, he's off again. *(Loudly, as before)* No bees in December. Not here. They're asleep. They go to sleep.

BILL: Susan, I'm Bill Windsor. Do you not remember me? Doctor Bill Windsor . . .

SUSAN: Doctor Windsor? Bill Windsor?

BILL: That's it. Well done.

SUSAN: Doctor Windsor, are you dead as well?

BILL: *(Laughing rather nervously)* No, no. Not as far as I know, anyway. We're both very much alive, Susan. This is your garden. You're in your garden . . .

SUSAN: My garden? This isn't my garden . . .

BILL: Yes, yes, it is. I promise you.

SUSAN: My garden's enormous. Five times the size of this, I can tell you . . . *(She tries to rise.)* Ah!

BILL: No, no. Don't try to sit up, not yet. Easy now, easy. Susan, you've apparently caught a bit of a knock on the head. You're going to feel a bit wobbly for a time so just stay put here . . .

SUSAN: Did I bang my head? How did I bang my head?

BILL: I think it was the old trick. You stood on the end of the garden rake. Nasty thing to happen.

SUSAN: *(Disgusted)* Typical of me. Typical.

BILL: I've—er—sent for an ambulance . . .

SUSAN: Ambulance? Oh, no, I don't need that.

BILL: I'd rather you did if you don't mind. The point is—blows to the head—you never can tell—could be a delayed reaction. Better safe than sorry. Probably just an overnight stop, that's all. Be back home here tomorrow. Right as rain. Probably.

SUSAN: Oh dear, what a nuisance.

BILL: There's a little bit of bruising—I had a quick look. Skin's not broken—probably have a nasty lump . . . Luckily it won't show much. Under the hair. Still they'll be able to tell at the hospital better than I can . . .

SUSAN: They're not going to need to shave my head, are they?

BILL: Good Lord, no. You're not going in for brain surgery. At least, I hope not. I'm afraid you'll have to wait for them, if you don't mind. The point is, I'm afraid I'm having a bit of trouble. With my bag there.

SUSAN: Trouble?

BILL: Yes, I can't get it open. The lock keeps jamming. I had an accident with it. In my car door. This morning. And. I mean I *can* get it open. In a real emergency. But it does entail a good deal of force in order to do so. And stuff tends to scatter. All over the place. So.

SUSAN: Oh, well. Please don't bother on my account.

BILL: Thanks.

(*A pause.* BILL *glances at his watch.* SUSAN *sits.*)

Well . . .

SUSAN: (*Sensing his unease*) You don't have to stay if you've—

BILL: No, no, no. Best for me to hang on. Just in case—things. Get.

(*He looks at his watch again.*)

Shouldn't be long. *(A sudden thought.)* Unless you'd like something. Would you like a glass of water?

SUSAN:  No, thank you.

BILL:  Tea? What about tea? Now, you'd like a cup of tea, wouldn't you?

SUSAN:  Well . . .

BILL:  I'll see if I can rustle up a cup of tea. Wait there. I'll do it. I'll also check to make sure she got that ambulance organized. Sit tight.

*(He moves away towards the unseen house.)*

*(Stopping suddenly to listen)* Someone else's not too happy by the sound of it . . .

SUSAN:  Sorry?

BILL:  The dog. Next door, is it?

SUSAN:  Dog?

BILL:  Howling. There. Can't you hear it? Hasn't stopped. Probably wants to be let in or—whoops—*(He trips and nearly falls.)*

SUSAN:  You all right?

BILL:  Yes, yes. Always doing that. Accident prone, that's me. You put it there, I'll fall over it. Back in a tick.

*(He goes.* SUSAN *sits alone for a moment. It is very quiet with none of the sounds one normally expects to hear in a suburban garden.)*

SUSAN:  *(To herself, puzzled)* Dog? I can't hear a dog . . .

*(In the distance,* ANDY'S *voice is heard. The garden grows imperceptibly bigger and lighter.)*

ANDY:  *(Off)* Susie . . . Susie, darling . . .

SUSAN:  *(Calling back)* I'm here, Andy. In the herb garden.

*(*ANDY *rushes on. A tall, good-looking, athletic man, easy-going and charming. He is perhaps a year or two younger than* SUSAN.*)*

ANDY:  Susie? I've just seen BIll Windsor. Are you all right?

SUSAN:  I'm perfectly fine, Andy. Just a silly accident, that's all.

ANDY:  *(Sitting beside her, immensely concerned)* Darling, what on earth happened? I can't leave you for five minutes, can I? What happened? He said you knocked yourself out . . .

SUSAN:  I just—banged my head. It's nothing, Andy, really. You mustn't fuss . . .

ANDY:  Of course I fuss. You're my wife. I love you. How on earth did you do it?

SUSAN:  I'm not even going to bring myself to tell you. It's so ridiculously silly . . .

ANDY:   I can't see what you can have banged your head on? Unless you stood on that garden . . . *(Seeing her face)* You didn't stand on the garden rake, darling?

SUSAN:   *(Mortified)* How could I have been so stupid?

ANDY:   *(Fairly amused but doing his best to conceal it)* Oh, you daft thing . . . *(He hugs her.)*

SUSAN:   *(Clinging to him)* It could only happen to someone like me . . .

ANDY:   We're all going to have to take extra special care of you, aren't we?

SUSAN:    . . . only someone this clumsy could have done it.

*(LUCY's voice is heard in the distance.)*

LUCY:   *(Off, calling)* Mummy! Daddy!

ANDY:   *(Calling)* Over here, chaps. In the herb garden. *(To* SUSAN*)* We'll soon nurse you better.

*(LUCY and TONY enter together. LUCY is a tall, good-looking, athletic girl, easy-going and charming. She is in her early twenties, and tends to wear fresh, summery, rather timeless dresses. TONY, on the other hand, is a tall, good-looking, athletic man, easy-going and charming. He is aged about thirty. Both appear to be midway through a game of tennis. TONY carries a glass of champagne.)*

LUCY:   Is Mother all right? Is she all right?

ANDY:   Don't panic. She'll be OK. She's OK.

SUSAN:   Nothing to worry about . . .

TONY:   What have you been up to now, Big Sis?

SUSAN:   Something quite ridiculous, I refuse to tell you. You'll only laugh . . .

LUCY:   *(Indignantly)* We won't laugh.

SUSAN:   Yes, you will. I know you two.

TONY:   *(Proffering the glass)* Here, drink this.

SUSAN:   What is it?

TONY:   Champers. I've only just opened it.

LUCY:   Champagne at eleven in the morning, I ask you. He's actually playing with the glass in his hand.

TONY:   The thing that's really annoying her is that I'm inflicting a crushing defeat as well. *(Offering* SUSAN *the glass)* Here. It is vintage.

ANDY:   Drink it, darling, it'll buck you up.

SUSAN:   Do you think I should?

ANDY:   Best possible thing, isn't it, Tony?

TONY:   Absolutely . . .

LUCY:   But what happened to Mother? I'm dying to know. How did she bang her head?

ANDY: Well . . .

SUSAN: Andy, don't you dare tell them. I'm not having them screaming with laughter at me . . .

LUCY: We're not going to scream with laughter. Are we, Tony?

TONY: Absolutely not.

SUSAN: Well, you might not, Lucy, but he's bound to.

ANDY: There's no big deal about it. All that happened—

SUSAN: Andy, don't you dare . . .

ANDY: —all that happened was, Susie went into the potting shed and the old tin bath in there slipped off the nail and fell on her . . .

LUCY: Gosh!

SUSAN: Thank you, darling. Thank you.

TONY: I loathe and detest tin baths . . .

ANDY: . . . and she was in such pain she came hopping out of the shed cursing and swearing and stepped on the garden rake . . . *(He laughs.)*

SUSAN: Andy! You beast!

(LUCY *and* TONY *laugh.*)

TONY: *(Laughing)* Stepped on the rake. I say . . .

LUCY: *(Laughing)*Honestly, Mummy, I didn't know people actually *did* that sort of thing . . .

SUSAN: I think you're all absolutely horrid and heartless.

ANDY: *(Taking command)* OK, kids. Joke's a joke. Lucy—

LUCY: Daddy?

ANDY: We must get your mother upstairs and into bed . . .

SUSAN: Oh, Andy, don't fuss—

ANDY: . . . Ask Mrs Simmonds to make a hot water bottle and light the fire in the master bedroom—

LUCY: Right. *(She turns to go.)*

ANDY: And give her a hand if she needs it. It's Ethel's day off—

LUCY: I'll see to it, Daddy.

ANDY: Good girl.

(LUCY *rushes off towards the house.*)

SUSAN: You really do spoil me, all of you . . .

ANDY: Nonsense.

TONY: We just want to get you fit so you can carry on slaving for us as usual.

ANDY:  *(Taking the empty glass from* SUSAN*)* Tony, get your sister another glass of this, will you?

SUSAN:  Andy, do you think I should? Bill Windsor's fetching some tea . . .

ANDY:  Tea? Oh, to hell with that . . .

TONY:  If it comes to a choice between Dom Perignon or Lapsang Souchong . . . Tell you what, I'll bring the ice bucket as well. You can pour it over your head.

(TONY *lopes off.*)

SUSAN:  *(Watching him go, affectionately)* He never alters, does he?

ANDY:  Not a tittle. Feel sorry for him in a way.

SUSAN:  Sorry? Why?

ANDY:  Well, mostly, when you get a brother and a sister like you two, things get shared. She gets the beauty, he gets the brains; or he gets the beauty, she gets the brains. Or even a bit for each of them. But with you and Tony, you've got the lot. All the brains, all the beauty. Hardly fair, is it?

SUSAN:  It's not true.

ANDY:  I'm afraid it is.

SUSAN:  But I love you for saying it, all the same. *(Starting to rise)* You can leave me now because I'm going to—*(She sways and nearly falls.)* Whoops!

ANDY: *(Catching her and helping her to sit again)* Steady! You are going to do nothing except sit here. As soon as Tony comes back, we're going to carry you up to bed.

SUSAN: *(Loving every minute of it)* Oh, Andy . . .

ANDY: Doctor's orders.

SUSAN: I think Bill Windsor's orders are that I go into hospital for a check-up.

ANDY: To blazes with that.

SUSAN: He's ordered an ambulance for me.

ANDY: Bill has?

SUSAN: Apparently.

ANDY: Oh, Lord. Hang on. *(He moves off.)*

SUSAN: Where are you going?

ANDY: To cancel it.

SUSAN: Cancel it?

ANDY: I don't want you in hospital, I want you here where we can look after you properly. Get you into that place, we'll never see you again—

SUSAN: *(Calling him back)* Andy . . .

ANDY: *(Turning back to her)* Hmmm?

SUSAN: Seriously. You do spoil me far too much.

ANDY: Maybe. I don't know. Perhaps. *(Returning to her)* If we do, I'll tell you why it is. Because we'd all be lost without you. There's only one of you, you see. *(Smiling slightly)* Unfortunately. And we all need you very much. Me most especially. I mean, after all, what does Tony stand to lose? Just a big sister. So what? Plenty of those. Ten a penny. And Lucy? Well—girls and their mothers. We all know what they're like. She'd soon get over it. But me? I'd be losing a wife. And that I'd never get over. Not one as dear and as precious as you.

*(He kisses her tenderly.)*

Whom, incidentally, I love more than words can ever say . . .

*(ANDY moves away and looking back on her smiles and leaves, blowing her the gentlest of kisses on one of his fingers. SUSAN stares after him. After a slight pause, she gives a little strangled moan of pleasure. BILL returns from the direction of the house. As he enters, he speaks to someone who has just passed him who, presumably, could have been ANDY. In the distance, briefly, a dog is heard howling to be let in.)*

BILL: *(Behind him)* . . . right, right, splendid. Did the trick, did it? *(Arriving, to SUSAN)* Sorry. Small delay. Trying to lend a hand in the kitchen. Fatal. Singed my sleeve. *(He sniffs his jacket.)* Ah, well. *(Sniffing the other sleeve)* I spilt liquid paraffin on this one, so it more or less evens it up . . . Feeling any better?

SUSAN: Much better, thank you.

BILL: Splendid. It's on its way. I just checked. The ambulance.

SUSAN: Ah. My husband hasn't spoken to you, then?

BILL: Your husband?

SUSAN: Yes. He seemed to feel I shouldn't go. He felt I'd be better off staying in bed here.

BILL: Really? When did he say this?

SUSAN: Just a minute ago.

BILL: Extraordinary. I mean, I didn't even know he was home. I understood he was on his way. He'd been telephoned and was on his way.

SUSAN: Well, he's here. He's just been talking to me.

BILL: How odd. Your sister-in-law obviously got it wrong.

SUSAN: My sister-in-law?

BILL: Yes—Marion, is it?

SUSAN: You mean my brother?

BILL: Muriel. That's it.

SUSAN: Tony.

BILL: Tony?

SUSAN: You mean my brother, Tony. Tall, fair, slim, good-looking in a rather weak sort of way . . .

BILL: No, definitely Muriel, Short, dark, angular, grim-looking in a rather firm sort of way . . . I haven't seen any Tony at all.

SUSAN: We don't have a Muriel. We have an Ethel but it's her day off. So it can't have been her.

BILL: Anyway, the woman in the kitchen. The one who made the tea.

SUSAN: Oh, that'll be Mrs Simmonds.

BILL: Mrs Muriel Simmonds?

SUSAN: I've no idea what her first name is, I've never asked her.

BILL: But Mrs Simmonds is your sister-in-law?

SUSAN: Certainly not, she's our cook.

BILL: Cook?

SUSAN: Yes. She's been with the family for—oh, ages and ages.

BILL: *(Very puzzled)* Has she? I see.

*(Pause.)*

She—er—seemed to be fairly convinced, in her own mind at least, that she was your sister-in-law.

SUSAN:  Did she?

BILL:  That's the distinct impression she gave.

SUSAN:  Well. She can be very strange. *(Pause.)* She's Cornish, I believe.

BILL:  Is she? One got the overall nuance from talking to her of someone from slightly nearer—South London. Anyway. The woman who found you lying in the garden, the woman who phoned me—or rather phoned your own doctor, Geoff Burgess, who happens to be on holiday, so you got his partner. Me. That woman.

SUSAN:  Possibly.

BILL:  The one who brought you out the tea. That one.

SUSAN:  Tea? What tea?

BILL:  Didn't you get the tea?

SUSAN:  Not yet. I thought you were bringing me some.

BILL:  No. She did. Her. Your Mrs Thing. I passed her just now. She was coming back with an empty cup in her hand.

SUSAN:  Really?

BILL:  So where did the tea go?

SUSAN:  Perhaps she drank it herself?

BILL:  She didn't come out here, then?

SUSAN:   I haven't seen her.

BILL:   No. Yes. I see.

*(He stares at her for a moment. He picks up his bag and struggles to open it for a moment. Then, aware that* SUSAN *is watching him, he puts it down.)*

SUSAN:   The only woman that I've seen all day has been my daughter.

BILL:   Oh, yes . . .

SUSAN:   She was playing tennis with Tony.

BILL:   Tennis?

SUSAN:   Yes.

BILL:   Where?

SUSAN:   *(Mildly exasperated)* On the tennis court.

BILL:   Which is—where exactly? From here?

SUSAN:   *(With enormous patience)* Over there.

BILL:   Ah, yes. Silly question.

*(He looks at his watch. The dog is howling again in the distance.)*

Any minute now. It'll be here.

SUSAN:   You know, I don't think you believe me, do you?

BILL: Yes, I do. No, no. Yes.

SUSAN: Why don't you believe me?

BILL: I do, I do. At least I believe that you believe it. It's just that I personally haven't seen hide nor hair of any of these people.

SUSAN: Well, that's hardly my fault, is it? *(Slight pause. Helpfully)* I can hear the dog now. If that's any help.

BILL: Good, good.

SUSAN: You can hear it, too, can't you? *(Anxiously)* You can hear it?

BILL: Oh, yes. *(Pause.)* No. I can't. I could but it stopped some time back.

SUSAN: Oh. There's something wrong with me, then, isn't there?

BILL: *(Cautiously)* I wouldn't say that . . .

SUSAN: Well, I suppose there could be with you . . .

BILL: No, I wouldn't say that either.

SUSAN: What would you say, then?

BILL: You—don't recall whether you've got a son by any chance, do you?

SUSAN: A son? Certainly not.

BILL: No?

SUSAN: Decidedly not. No, that I would remember. Well, I'd hardly forget whether or not I had a son, would I?

BILL: No. It's just—well, I'm not your regular doctor, as I say—

SUSAN: *(Impatiently)* I know that. I remember, perfectly.

BILL: But I have called on you and your—family in the past. To see your husband. And your—son. On one or two occasions. I think chicken-pox was one. I can't be certain about that.

SUSAN: *(Coolly)* You're obviously muddling me up with somebody else.

BILL: *(Rather significantly)* No, that's not all that likely, believe me.

*(A pause.)*

These—tennis courts that you can see . . . ?

SUSAN: I can't see them.

BILL: You can't?

SUSAN: No. Can you?

BILL: No. That's not the point. The point is, can you?

SUSAN: Of course I can't.

BILL:  Good. Splendid.

SUSAN:  They're round the back of the house.

BILL:  Oh.

(Pause.)

SUSAN:  I can see the swimming pool, if that's any help?

BILL:  Ah.

SUSAN:  And the lawn. And the rose beds and—yes—look, if you stand here on tiptoe you can just see the lake. Look.

BILL:  (Humouring her, straining to look) Uh-huh. Uh-huh.

SUSAN:  Doesn't it look beautiful today? It's always best in the late afternoon sun.

BILL:  Yes, yes. (He consults his watch again.)

(A pause.)

Yes.

SUSAN:  (Watching him) You can't see any of it, can you?

BILL:  I see—a small garden—very pleasant, very tidy, about 20 feet wide by maybe about 30 foot long . . . There's a little pond over there. Not a lot in it—a stone frog, is it?—I think it's a frog—the thing I fell over, anyway. Some flowerbeds with wallflowers—shrubs, several shrubs—one newly planted. Presumably by you. A rockery there—

SUSAN:  Please don't go on.

BILL:  What?

SUSAN:  I don't want to listen to any more of this.

BILL:  *(Gently)* I'm afraid it's what's here.

SUSAN:  You're describing some place I wouldn't choose to live in, even in my wildest nightmares.

BILL:  Oh, I am sorry.

*(A silence.)*

SUSAN:  My brother brought me some champagne, you know.

BILL:  Did he? Jolly nice.

SUSAN:  Dom Perignon. Vintage 1978.

BILL:  That's the stuff, eh? *(Laughing awkwardly)* He didn't leave any behind, did he?

SUSAN:  *(Frostily)* I think it would be better if you went, doctor.

BILL:  Oh, I'm not sure that would—

SUSAN:  It's all right. I'll arrange an appointment with Doctor Burgess—

BILL:  He's on holiday—

SUSAN:   —as soon as he returns . . .

BILL:   —for a fortnight. In Spain.

SUSAN:   Thank you so much for your help. Good afternoon.

BILL:   Look, it's not the afternoon, it's eleven-fifteen in the morning and I really cannot leave you—

SUSAN:   I'm only waiting here for my husband, that's all. I'm not going to do anything foolish.

BILL:   But you will go in the ambulance, won't you?

SUSAN:   No.

BILL:   Ah. Now. I'm sorry. I really must insist you do.

SUSAN:   Not unless my husband is agreeable.

BILL:   Right, fine. Fair enough. We'll hang on for him then, shall we?

SUSAN:   If you like. I don't think he will agree. In fact I'm only waiting here because he insists on carrying me up to bed.

BILL:   Splendid.

(*He gathers up his bag.* SUSAN *wanders away slightly and gazes out.*)

SUSAN:   Just look at the rose garden today. A mass of pinks and reds and yellows . . .

(BILL *stands waiting for a second.* SUSAN *continues to stare at her garden.*)

BILL: *(Hearing something)* Ah, here they come, I do believe.

SUSAN: Good. Now perhaps you'll believe me.

BILL: *(To someone off in the distance)* Hallo, good afternoon. *(Turning to her)* Mrs Gannet? Susan? Remember them now? Your husband and your sister-in-law? *(Gently)* Mrs Gannet . . .

SUSAN: *(Turning)* Who on earth's Mrs Gannet when she's—?

(*As she speaks and turns, her real family enters. She breaks off. She stares at the two who have just entered. First, the* REVEREND GERALD GANNET, *a solemn man in his middle forties. With him his sister,* MURIEL, *much as described by* BILL *earlier. She is a woman who has known her share of suffering and is anxious others should know about it too. Certainly, as seen through* SUSAN'S *(and therefore to a large extent our own) eyes, the two present an unattractive picture, entirely lacking the lightness and ease of her earlier family.*)

GERALD: Hallo, dear.

MURIEL: Another cup of tea, Susan?

(SUSAN *looks at them in horror. Her knees buckle, she gives a terrible moan and falls into a faint causing a blackout. There is the briefest of pauses. Then we hear* SUSAN'S *cry as she jolts awake with a start. The lights come up abruptly. We are still in the garden. It is morning again.* SUSAN *is seated in a garden chair. Another couple of chairs are also in evidence.* GERALD *is standing nearby. It is he, apparently, who has woken her.*)

GERALD:  Were you asleep?

SUSAN:  *(Shaking herself awake)* Yes, I must have—must have dozed off . . .

GERALD:  It's eleven-thirty. I thought you should know.

SUSAN:  Why?

GERALD:  Rick's here for lunch.

SUSAN:  Yes, I know. You told me.

(GERALD *paces round the garden rather restlessly.*)

GERALD:  There is a school of thought that believes that sleep is for the night. You seem to be out to disprove them—Is that bush dead? It looks dead from here.

SUSAN:  I'd sleep at night if I could. I'm finding it very difficult recently . . .

GERALD:  Hardly surprising. If you sleep all day.

SUSAN:  *(Rather irritably)* What do you want, Gerald? Do you want me to do something for you?

GERALD:  No, no. Don't stir yourself on my account. I was just taking a brief break from the book. Thought I'd see what you were doing. Now I know. Sleeping.

SUSAN:  Might I remind you, I only came out of hospital this morning.

GERALD:  Presumably they released you because they considered you fit and well. Anyway, Bill Windsor just phoned. Said he'd look in later.

SUSAN:    Oh, he doesn't have to bother . . .

GERALD:    Ask him for a tablet or something. To help you sleep. At night. Or perhaps a stimulant. To keep you awake. In the daytime.

SUSAN:    Has it ever occurred to you why I can't sleep at nights?

GERALD:    Insomnia?

SUSAN:    Perhaps it's because I'm not very happy, Gerald.

GERALD:    Well, who is? These days. Very few.

SUSAN:    You seem happy.

GERALD:    Do I? Maybe I'm just better at hiding these things. Who knows?

SUSAN:    At least you sleep at night.

GERALD:    Only because I'm exhausted from a full day's work. I give my body no option.

SUSAN:    Zonk.

GERALD:    I beg your pardon?

SUSAN:    You just zonk out.

GERALD:  I've no idea what that means. Zonk? There's your solution. Fill your day a bit more. Then you'll sleep.

SUSAN:  *(Flaring)* I work extremely hard, Gerald, and you know it. I help you whenever I'm able. I run this house for you—

GERALD:  With the help of my sister, you do—

SUSAN:  No, Gerald, *despite* Muriel's help, I run this house. I do all the cooking, the bulk of the washing up, *all* the laundry—including Muriel's—I cope with the sheer boring slog of tidying up after both of you, day after day, I make the beds, I—

GERALD:  All right. All right, dear. We don't need the catalogue. All I'm saying is—you still don't seem to have enough to do.

SUSAN:  No, you're absolutely right, Gerald. I don't. Not nearly enough. Not any more.

GERALD:  Something the matter?

SUSAN:  There must be. I don't know what my role is these days. I don't any longer know what I'm supposed to be doing. I used to be a wife. I used to be a mother. And I loved it. People said, Oh, don't you long to get out and do a proper job? And I'd say, No thanks, this is a proper job, thank you. Mind your own business. But now it isn't any more. The thrill has gone.

GERALD:  Oh, we're back on that, are we?

SUSAN:  'Fraid so . . .

GERALD: 'The trivial round, the common task,
Will furnish all we need to ask . . .'

SUSAN: Yes, it's usually about now that you come up with that invaluable piece of advice, Gerald. The point is it's not true. They don't. Furnish. All we need to ask. Not on their own. Whoever wrote it was talking through his hat. Anyway, how can you possibly believe anybody who rhymes 'road' with 'God' . . .

GERALD: All one can say is that they're words that have provided comfort to several generations . . .

SUSAN: Good-o.

GERALD: *(Suddenly irritated by her)* If you want something to do, why don't you pull up that dead bush?

SUSAN: It's not dead. I planted it yesterday. In between hitting myself on the head . . .

GERALD: How is the head?

SUSAN: Fine. The bump's going down. Scarcely feel it.

*(A silence. GERALD walks about again.)*

GERALD: Bill Windsor was telling me you'd been—hallucinating.

SUSAN: Was he?

GERALD: Apparently you saw people. Is that so?

SUSAN: I thought doctors were supposed to treat things in confidence . . .

GERALD: He told me. I'm your husband. He felt I should know. In case it happened again. Has it happened again?

SUSAN: No.

GERALD: *(Amused by this)* What sort of people did you see? Were they nice? I hope so.

SUSAN: Very nice, thank you. Most attractive and dishy.

GERALD: It was a—sexual—thing, then, was it?

SUSAN: No.

GERALD: No?

SUSAN: Not really.

GERALD: Was—was I there?

SUSAN: No, you were not. Nobody I knew was there. Except for Bill Windsor, of course . . .

GERALD: Bill Windsor? Good Lord, do you mean you were fantasizing over Bill Windsor?

SUSAN: No. Bill was just there.

GERALD: What was he doing?

SUSAN: Nothing much. Struggling with his bag. Falling over frogs . . .

GERALD: Much the same as he does in real life.

SUSAN: It was real life.

GERALD: I thought you said this was a fantasy?

SUSAN: It was. Bill was real. The rest was a fantasy. Oh, I can't explain it. You wouldn't understand, anyway.

GERALD: I don't know. Some would say, that for a man in my line of business, it was very much up his street. (He laughs at this.) I mean as a specialist in matters unseen . . .

SUSAN: Yes, all right, Gerald. That's a jolly good joke . . .

GERALD: But I can't be of help in your case?

SUSAN: We've known each other rather a long time, haven't we?

GERALD: Said by anybody else, that could have been interpreted as quite an affectionate remark. Spoken by you, it sounds like an appalling accusation.

SUSAN: (Offhandedly) Well, you know I don't love you any more, Gerald. You knew that.

GERALD: Yes. I did know. (Pause.) I don't think you've ever said it—quite so baldly as that before—but I got the message . . .

SUSAN: I'm still reasonably fond of you.

GERALD: Yes?

SUSAN: Most of the time. Well, don't look so glum. You don't love me, either.

GERALD: Yes, I do.

SUSAN: Oh. Come on . . .

GERALD: I do. At least, I'm not aware that my feelings towards you have altered that much—

SUSAN: What? Not at all?

GERALD: Not that I'm aware of—

SUSAN: Oh, Gerald—

GERALD: I still feel the same—

SUSAN: We don't kiss—we hardly touch each other—we don't make love—we don't even share the same bed now. We sleep at different ends of the room—

GERALD: That's just sex you're talking about. That's just the sexual side—

SUSAN: Well, of course it is—

GERALD: There's more to it than that, surely?

SUSAN: Not at the moment there isn't.

GERALD: You mean that the—sex—is the only thing that's mattered to you in our relationship?

SUSAN: Of course not.

GERALD:   That's what you seem to be saying.

SUSAN:   What I'm saying is . . . All I'm saying is, that once that's gone—all *that*—it becomes important. Over-important, really. I mean before, when we—it was just something else we did together. Like gardening. Only now I have to do that on my own as well. It was something we shared. A couple of times a week. Or whatever—

GERALD:   More than that. More than that.

SUSAN:   Yes. Whatever. The point is that then, everything else, the everyday bits, just ticked along nicely. But take that away, the really joyous part of us—and everything else rather loses its purpose. That's all.

*(A pause.)*

GERALD:   What you're really saying is, that I've let you down. Failed to deliver. Is that it?

SUSAN:   That's not what I mean. It's nobody's fault. It just happened, over the years.

GERALD:   My fault. I see.

SUSAN:   I knew you'd say that.

GERALD:   That's how you make it sound, anyway.

*(He paces about.)*

I rather thought you'd lost interest in all that, you know.

*(She does not answer.)*

I thought that when a woman got to—our age—she more or less . . . switched off.

SUSAN:   Yes, well, I'm a freak, Gerald. I'm afraid you married a freak . . .

(MURIEL *comes from the house at this moment bearing a tray with some dubious-looking cups of coffee.*)

MURIEL:   I thought I'd make some coffee. Since nobody else was . . .

GERALD:   (*Now full of bonhomie*) Ah, bless you, Muriel.

(SUSAN *has closed her eyes.*)

Muriel's made us a nice cup of coffee, dear.

SUSAN:   Goody, goody, goody . . .

MURIEL:   I hope it's all right. Susan generally manages to find something wrong with my coffee . . . I'd have thought she'd have made some herself by now, rather than leaving it to me . . .

(SUSAN *ignores them.*)

GERALD:   (*In a loud whisper*) She's in a little tiny bit of a mood, Muriel. Don't worry.

MURIEL:   (*Whispering in turn*) Oh. Do you want me to go?

GERALD:   Heavens, no. Stay here. Sit here with us. You can help cheer things up.

(SUSAN *makes a mirthless, laughing sound.* MURIEL *sits down with them.*)

MURIEL:  This garden could do with a tidy, couldn't it? That bush is dead.

SUSAN:  *(Eyes closed)* You're welcome to take over any time, Muriel.

MURIEL:  I wouldn't dare. Not after last time. I learnt my lesson. She went on and on at me . . .

SUSAN:  Because you stuck a garden fork through the bottom of the pond—

MURIEL:  I did no such thing—

SUSAN:  You murdered my goldfish, Muriel. I shall never forgive you.

GERALD:  This is an interesting cup of coffee, Muriel.

MURIEL:  Nice?

GERALD:  Very interesting. Yes.

SUSAN:  *(Examining her cup for the first time)* What powder did you use?

MURIEL:  Here we go, the Spanish Inquisition—

SUSAN:  I was only curious—

MURIEL:  I used the coffee in the tin marked Coffee. All right?

GERALD: That sounds logical to me . . .

SUSAN: Yes, it is. Fairly. This is the ready-ground coffee, Muriel, not the instant . . .

MURIEL: I don't know what sort it is. If you don't want it, I'll take it back . . .

GERALD: No, no, this is perfect, Muriel. First rate.

MURIEL: *(Muttering)* Can't do anything right, can I?

SUSAN: Delicious, Muriel. You must give me the secret.

GERALD: Susan, now . . .

MURIEL: *(Muttering)* I don't know what she's talking about, I'm sure. You just put it in a cup and pour water over it, don't you?

GERALD: Perfect. *(He smiles at* MURIEL.*)*

*(Pause.)*

MURIEL: I don't know why I'm suddenly this terrible cook. Why I'm suddenly made to feel so incompetent. I nursed our mother perfectly satisfactorily for her last twelve years . . .

GERALD: True, true . . . You gave away your prime, Muriel.

MURIEL: I did. And my dear, late, bedridden husband Harry for another seven. I cooked three meals a day, seven days a week, three hundred and sixty-five days a year for that man until the day he died . . .

GERALD: *(Murmuring)* Yes. Amazing. Amazing.

MURIEL: So. I didn't do so badly.

SUSAN: I've no doubt you'll see us all off as well, Muriel.

MURIEL: *(Indignantly)* Well . . .

GERALD: That's a very unfeeling remark, Susan . . .

SUSAN: Sorry.

GERALD: In view of Muriel's past and present sufferings and tribulations, I think the least you can do is make allowances . . .

SUSAN: Sorry, sorry, sorry . . .

MURIEL: Got out of bed the wrong side this morning, didn't she?

SUSAN: Fat chance of that. It's over the other side of the room.

GERALD: Now, now, now . . .

*(Pause.)*

MURIEL: I didn't sleep again.

GERALD: *(Sympathetically)* No?

MURIEL:  I felt him very close again last night . . .

GERALD:  Harry, this is?

MURIEL:  At one point, I sensed him—even though my eyes were closed—bending over me, gazing into my face. I felt his breath on my cheek. And the room went deathly cold. Do you think it's possible, Gerald, that he's trying to get back to me?

GERALD:  Well frankly, Muriel, I have to be honest. I don't hold out all that hope. I have to say that . . .

MURIEL:  But he's still there, Gerald . . .

GERALD:  Oh, yes, I'm sure he's there, Muriel. I'm certain he's there. Somewhere. It's just really the nature of where is *there*. You see I don't think that *there* is necessarily *here*. If you follow.

MURIEL:  No . . .

SUSAN:  Extremely unlikely, I'd have thought.

MURIEL:  *(Coolly)* I don't know what you know about these things, Susan.

SUSAN:  Nothing at all. But it does seem to me that God, in his infinite wisdom and with the entire cosmos to choose from is unlikely to base the Kingdom of Heaven around Muriel's bedroom . . .

GERALD:  That is not only facetious, Susan, that is also blasphemous.

SUSAN: I'm sorry, Gerald.

GERALD: I hardly think that it's me you should be apologizing to.

SUSAN: Sorry, God.

GERALD: I actually meant to Muriel.

SUSAN: Oh, rather. Let's get our priorities right. Muriel, then God, then Gerald. I've got it. Sorry, Muriel.

(GERALD *opens his mouth to speak, then thinks better of it. A silence.*)

GERALD: *(Not moving)* Well, I think I must . . . Back to the book.

MURIEL: My dear friend Enid Armitage—when she lost her fiancé in the rail crash of 1959 . . .

GERALD: I remember. I remember your friend Enid . . .

MURIEL: She willed her Desmond back to her. She willed him back. Every night, before she went to sleep, every night for three and a half years she concentrated on Desmond's image, willing him back. Not that she ever saw him. But one morning she woke up, she opened her eyes and there, on the bedroom ceiling, written in this dark sort of chalky substance: 'LOVE . . . ENID . . . ETERNALLY . . .'

GERALD: Yes, I do remember it. It caused quite a sensation.

MURIEL:  Written there in a chalky substance. Over her head when she woke.

GERALD:  Yes. *(Pause.)* I recall, though, that they did establish it was Enid's handwriting, didn't they?

MURIEL:  Oh, yes. But then he worked through her hand, didn't he? Desmond made use of her hand . . .

SUSAN:  *(Murmuring)* I hope he put it back when he'd finished with it . . .

MURIEL:  *(Ignoring this)* And remember this. They never did find that chalk, did they?

GERALD:  Perfectly true.

MURIEL:  *(Half to herself)* LOVE . . . ENID . . . ETERNALLY . . .

GERALD:  You going to sleep again, Susan?

SUSAN:  Not quite . . .

GERALD:  Well, don't forget Rick's here for lunch, will you?

SUSAN:  So you keep saying.

MURIEL:  We didn't get a lot of notice, did we?

GERALD:  Oh, you know what Rick's like. I only got his letter this morning . . .

MURIEL:  We should be getting things ready, shouldn't we? If Rick's coming. I mean I'd do it but I don't like to do it.

SUSAN: Don't bother. He won't want anything to eat. Just a few nuts and berries from the hedgerow . . .

GERALD: He'll need something. He's coming from Hemel Hempstead.

SUSAN: I'll put him out a glass of rainwater, then.

GERALD: Your usual motherly self, I see.

SUSAN: Well, he's hardly particularly filial, is he? We haven't seen him for two years . . .

GERALD: *(Wearily)* You know why that is. This particular philosophical group—

SUSAN: Now he won't even speak to us . . .

GERALD: That's just one of their rules, that's all. Heavens, theirs isn't the first example of a silent order. Think of the Cistercians . . .

SUSAN: They were slightly less discriminating. I mean, correct me if I'm wrong, but Trappists aren't just forbidden to talk to their parents, are they?

MURIEL: I don't know what you know about these things, Susan, I'm sure.

GERALD: He still writes letters, doesn't he? Very newsworthy letters . . .

SUSAN: He does. To you.

GERALD:  That's the way they are. The boys write to their fathers, the girls write to their mothers . . .

SUSAN:  Girls? You mean they've got girls joining now?

GERALD:  One or two, I believe.

SUSAN:  *(Laughing)* That'll terrify the life out of Ricky.

GERALD:  Nonsense.

SUSAN:  The only reason he joined, so far as I can make out, was to avoid meeting women.

GERALD:  Don't be so ridiculous—

SUSAN:  They frighten the life out of him.

GERALD:  *(Stung by this slur on his son)* If they do, I think we can easily see the cause.

SUSAN:  Me?

GERALD:  Oh, yes . . .

SUSAN:  I hardly ever saw the boy. You bullied him into that scholarship and then packed him off to that piddling little public school where he never saw anything female aged under fifty-five or weighing less than fifteen stone till the day he left . . .

GERALD:  Let's not get into this, Susan.

SUSAN:  You forget I used to have to listen to his prayers every night of his holidays, Gerald. 'Please God, don't make me have to get married.'

GERALD:  That is nonsense—

SUSAN:  That's what he used to say . . .

MURIEL:  I don't know what you know about these things, Susan . . .

SUSAN:  Poor little sod. Sixteen years old and, until I told him, he thought his bed got damp in the night because the roof leaked. You did nothing for him, Gerald. Nothing. He could have died for all you cared. And now he's grown up he won't even speak to me—(*She breaks off, suddenly very tearful.*)

(*A silence. The dog starts howling in the distance.*)

MURIEL:  (*Starting to gather up the cups*) If we've all finished, I'll . . . clear these up . . .

GERALD:  Yes. I must get on. Do another half hour on the book.

MURIEL:  Shall I bring you another cup, Gerald?

GERALD:  (*Rather hastily*) No, Muriel, no, thank you. Don't want to spoil my lunch.

MURIEL:  Hark at that poor little dog, isn't it terrible? Why doesn't she let him in when he howls like that?

GERALD:   I think old Mrs Ogle's just a little bit deaf, Muriel, that's the problem . . .

MURIEL:   Well, she ought to do something about it, oughtn't she?

SUSAN:   *(Savagely)* Like shoot it . . .

(MURIEL *tuts at this and goes off with the cups towards the house.* GERALD *hovers awkwardly, feeling something more need be said.)*

GERALD:   He always sends his love, you know. Rick. When he writes. He always sends you his love.

SUSAN:   Does he? You must send mine back then, mustn't you?

GERALD:   Yes, I usually do. When I write. Well.

*(At this point,* LUCY, *now in a light, flowing summer dress comes chasing past them laughing. The sound is very faint.* TONY *comes on in pursuit. They chase off.* SUSAN *watches them.)*

(GERALD *looks at* SUSAN, *puzzled.)*

What is it?

SUSAN:   Nothing.

GERALD:   You looked as though you'd seen something?

SUSAN:   Only a bee.

GERALD:   A bee?

SUSAN:  A December bee.

GERALD:  *(Seeing someone approaching)* Ah, here he is. Bill
Windsor's arrived. *(Calling)* Morning, Bill!

(BILL *arrives, tripping as he comes.*)

BILL:  Hallo, there—whoops—

GERALD:  *(Laughing)* Careful, Bill, careful . . .

BILL:  *(Looking at what he tripped over)* That's my friend the
frog again, I think. Is it a frog?

SUSAN:  It was.

BILL:  And how are things here—? Good morning, Susan.

SUSAN:  Hallo.

BILL:  How are you today?

GERALD:  Well, the bump's gone you'll be glad to hear—

BILL:  Has it? Good, good. I hoped it would. Any more hallucinations?

GERALD:  Apparently not.

BILL:  Splendid.

GERALD:  No more visitations.

BILL:  Ah, that's healthy. How's she sleeping?

GERALD:  Well, that's a bit more of a problem. She's not getting her sleep at nights, at all . . .

BILL:  Oh, dear . . .

GERALD:  So she's tending to drop off during the day. Which isn't the way, of course . . .

BILL:  No, no. I think I might prescribe her a mild sedative then, Gerald. She's not allergic to that sort of thing, is she?

GERALD:  No, no . . . I don't think so.

BILL:  Right. *(Leaning in to* SUSAN, *confidentially)* Everything else working normally, is it? Waterworks? Other bits?

SUSAN:  I've no idea. You'd better ask my husband.

BILL:  *(Puzzled)* Sorry?

SUSAN:  *(Moving away from them)* I'm fine now, Bill, absolutely fine . . .

GERALD:  Don't forget Rick's here for lunch, will you, dear?

SUSAN:  *(With a flashing smile)* Oh, heavens above! Thank you for reminding me, I practically forgot.

BILL:  Rick? That's your son, Rick? *(He looks at* SUSAN *for confirmation.)*

SUSAN:  Yes. I remember him now. It's all right.

BILL:  Good, good. You keeping busy, Gerald?

(SUSAN *moves away from the men and wanders a little as they talk, half listening to them.*)

GERALD:   Well . . . just finishing off the book, you know.

BILL:   Really? Are you on a book? Bursting into print, are you? Clever chap.

GERALD:   *(Modestly)* Well, it's a small little venture. Nothing earth-shattering. I was commissioned by the Civic Society —it's a short history of the parish. For the centenary, you know.

BILL:   Oh, you mean next year's shindig?

GERALD:   That's the one. Just a few thousand words, you know. Trying to condense six hundred years into sixty pages . . .

BILL:   Well, I take my hat off to you. I doubt I even know a few thousand words. Let alone start writing them down. Unless you're allowed to repeat some?

(*They laugh and move further away from* SUSAN.)

GERALD:   *(His voice fading away as they move out of earshot)* I'll tell you what I've been wanting to ask you, Bill. It's whether . . .

(*As* GERALD *is speaking,* LUCY *enters and comes to* SUSAN, *carrying two glasses of champagne. The men, naturally, are unaware of her and continue a silent conversation of their own.*)

LUCY:   Mummy, Daddy says lunch will be ready in fifteen

minutes and you're to drink this because you still look far too pale and interesting . . .

SUSAN:  Oh, Lucy, I'll be legless if I do—

LUCY:  Good. I'll join you. *(Raising her glass)* Here's to the family!

SUSAN:  *(Responding)* The family!

*(They drink.)*

Is Daddy coping in the kitchen?

LUCY:  Of course he is. He's being his ace super chef. Everybody stand back. He's making that wonderful salmon dish with his own special mayonnaise. And I think he's made summer pudding and some homemade peach sorbet—Oh, just mountains and mountains as usual. Enough for an army . . .

SUSAN:  He never learns . . .

LUCY:  And Tony and I have volunteered to tidy up after him—which should take us the rest of the afternoon. Meanwhile you are allowed just to lounge around here getting as legless as you like.

SUSAN:  No, that's not good enough, I've got work to do as well, you know —

LUCY:  On your book? Super. How's it coming?

SUSAN:  *(With a quiet confidence)* All right, I think. I've done all the slog, all the heavy research, now I can actually get down to real writing . . .

LUCY:    I think you're amazing. I don't know how you do it.

SUSAN:    *(Shrugging)* Well . . .

LUCY:    We're just all so proud of you, Mummy, you've no idea. I know you won't read these things, but did you know that last Sunday in the *Observer*, they called you probably our most important living historical novelist . . .

SUSAN:    Did they, darling? Well . . . it was the *Observer*— The point is, darling, I don't think that any writer can take—

*(She breaks off as GERALD hails her from a distance.)*

GERALD:    Dearest, Bill says he'll stop for lunch. All right?

SUSAN:    Fine.

GERALD:    We'll have enough, won't we?

SUSAN:    Mountains.

BILL:    Thank you—

SUSAN:    *(Softly)* Salmon and summer pudding and sorbet . . .

BILL:    Sorry?

SUSAN:    It'll only be frozen quiche, I'm afraid.

BILL: Oh, first class. We live on them.

GERALD: You all right, darling?

SUSAN: Yes.

GERALD: What were you doing?

SUSAN: Trying to remember a poem . . .

GERALD: It's twenty to one . . . Don't forget—? No.

(GERALD *and* BILL *resume their tête-à-tête. They are evidently now talking about* SUSAN. *Shortly, under the next, unnoticed by* SUSAN *they both go off to the house.* SUSAN *returns her attention to* LUCY *who has been sitting, throughout the last, deep in thought.*)

LUCY: Mummy, now I've got you on my own, there's something I desperately want to tell you—

SUSAN: What's that, darling?

LUCY: It's just that I've met someone I love very much and we want to get married.

SUSAN: *(Touched)* Oh, darling.

LUCY: Are you upset?

SUSAN: Upset? Why should I be upset?

LUCY: You're crying . . .

SUSAN: That's only— That's only because I'm so happy for you—

LUCY: *(Hugging her)* Oh, Mummy. *(Now very excited and bubbling)* He's amazing. You'll love him, too. I know you will. He's witty and charming and handsome and tender—

SUSAN: I know, I know he will be—

LUCY: You know? How?

SUSAN: Oh, I just know. When can I meet him?

LUCY: Soon. May I invite him round?

SUSAN: Of course—

LUCY: I hope Daddy likes him—

SUSAN: He will.

LUCY: And Tony. I want you all to like him.

SUSAN: They will. We'll make sure they do. You and me.

LUCY: Yes. That's why I told you first. And I always will. I'll tell you everything first. I promise.

SUSAN: Thank you, darling . . .

LUCY: Now. More champers?

(SUSAN *looks doubtful.*)

You must. To drink my health.

SUSAN: All right. Just one more.

Stockard Channing

Remak Ramsay, Stockard Channing and Simon Jones

Remak Ramsay and Stockard Channing

Tracy Pollan, Michael Countryman, Daniel Gerroll and Stockard Channing

LUCY:    *(Scrambling away)* I'll be back soon . . .

(LUCY *goes, taking* SUSAN's *glass.* SUSAN *watches her for a second.)*

SUSAN:    *(With a sudden thought)* Oh, Lord. Lunch. What am I doing?

*(She makes to leave, passing* BILL *as he returns.)*

BILL:    Hallo. Where are you off to?

SUSAN:    Do excuse me, I should have started lunch. Sorry, I got carried away with something else.

BILL:    Hey, well, no, wait. It's all right. It's all under control.

SUSAN:    *(Stopping)* Is it?

BILL:    I've just been telling Gerald that, in my view, you're still not a hundred per cent. You've got to take it easier, you know.

SUSAN:    No, I'm better, really.

BILL:    One more day taking things quietly. That's all. Promise. Won't do you any harm. For me.

SUSAN:    Well. We won't get any lunch.

BILL:    Your sister-in-law was delighted to take over.

SUSAN:    Was she? I bet.

BILL:    She's going to fix us all a light snack.

SUSAN: Light?

BILL: Omelettes, apparently.

SUSAN: Oh, yes, I remember them. There is—this frozen quiche if you'd prefer it.

BILL: No. An omelette aux fines herbes sounds rather delicious.

SUSAN: Yes, doesn't it sound it . . .

BILL: Hope you don't mind me gatecrashing. I'm afraid I more or less invited myself. I didn't intend to. Nora, my wife, she's away at the moment, you see. Having a well-earned holiday. In Portugal. So I'm afraid I'm scrounging meals where I can.

SUSAN: You may live to regret it. At least, I hope you will. Live I mean.

(BILL *laughs.* LUCY *enters during the next with a glass of champagne.*)

BILL: Gerald was telling me that— Shall we sit down?

SUSAN: Yes, of course.

(BILL *adjusts the chairs.* SUSAN *notices* LUCY.)

(*To* LUCY) Just put it there, darling, thank you.

LUCY: Right.

BILL: Right you are.

(LUCY *goes.* BILL *plonks the chair down as instructed.*)

That all right for you there?

SUSAN:   Thank you. *(Sitting)* Did I—? Did I say something just then?

BILL:   When?

SUSAN:   While you were moving the chairs?

BILL:   Er—yes. You said—just put it there. Darling.

SUSAN:   I did?

BILL:   Did you—not know you'd said it?

SUSAN:   Yes, I knew I'd said it. I was just checking if you'd heard it. You had.

BILL:   Yes. I had. *(He smiles at her.)*

*(Pause.)*

No more hallucinations, I hope?

SUSAN:   No. No. *(Slight pause.)* No.

BILL:   Sure?

SUSAN:   Positive.

BILL:   These things can linger on, you see. Sometimes. Do you get much of a chance to relax at all? Any hobbies, that sort of thing?

SUSAN:  Not really. I watch far too much television, if you call that relaxing.

BILL:  Oh, yes. Rather. Best sleeping draught there is.

SUSAN:  The problem is I watch such trash most of the time, I just sit there feeling guilty. Saying to myself, what on earth am I doing watching *this?* Why aren't I watching something useful? I mean, I do try sometimes to watch interesting programmes but I find them all so boring. I read a bit.

BILL:  Good, good.

SUSAN:  Not the right books, of course. Historical romances, that sort of thing.

BILL:  Ah.

SUSAN:  I can see you thoroughly disapprove.

BILL:  Not at all. What's a *right* book, for heaven's sake? I read science fiction.

SUSAN:  Do you?

BILL:  All the time.

SUSAN:  Well. I don't feel so bad then.

BILL:  Do you play any sports?

SUSAN:  Good Lord, no.

BILL: Not a bad idea. To take up something. It doesn't have to be squash.

SUSAN: I—I did think about riding. Learning to ride. But I think it's a bit late at my age. Sitting astride some aged, minute pony with hundreds of giggling seven-year-olds looking on. I desperately wanted a horse when I was young but . . .

BILL: Couldn't you?

SUSAN: No, my father didn't approve.

BILL: Of horses?

SUSAN: Of animals. Dogs, cats, hamsters, horses. He had a theory that they gave off diseases . . .

BILL: Well, he was right, they do. They also give off an awful lot of happiness. Which probably balances it up in the long run. People may catch diseases but at least they die happier. So no horse?

SUSAN: No. No pets at all.

BILL: Shame.

*(The conversation seems to have lowered* SUSAN's *spirits somewhat.)*

*(Changing the subject)* Your husband was telling me about his book. Sounds a cracker.

SUSAN: What, his history of the parish since 1386? Yes.

BILL:  Going to be very interesting, I'd have thought.

SUSAN:  Oh, yes.

BILL:  Fascinating.

SUSAN:  But only to people who've lived here.

BILL:  Oh, yes.

SUSAN:  Preferably since 1386.

BILL:  What? Oh. *(He laughs.)* Lot of hard work.

SUSAN:  Oh, yes. *(Pause.)* Actually, Gerald's been working on it since 1386.

(BILL *laughs a lot at this one.*)

BILL:  1386 . . . yes. *(Pause.)* Your son's due shortly.

SUSAN:  Yes.

BILL:  He's your one-and-only, isn't he?

SUSAN:  Yes. Our one-and-only. We'd probably have had more if it hadn't been for my husband's book—

BILL:  Oh, yes?

SUSAN:  That's tended to burn up most of his midnight oils. If you follow me.

BILL:  *(Philosophically)* Ah, well. I know how these things can get you. Hobbies and so on. I'm—er—I'm actually into macramé, would you believe? You know, the old knotted string bit.

SUSAN: Really? I'd never have thought of you doing that. How clever.

BILL: I'm still at rather early stages, I'm afraid. I spend most of the night unpicking it. But Nora's all for it. Well, she introduced me to it. Very encouraging. She's even let me have the spare bedroom.

(GERALD *enters. In one hand, he has a tray with a dusty bottle of sherry and some assorted glasses. In his other hand, a small folding card table.*)

GERALD: The sum total of our drink supply appears to be a bottle of Marsala. I don't know if anyone cares for Marsala.

BILL: Marsala. Well, that sounds like a challenge. Why not?

GERALD: *(Struggling)* Thank you, Bill. If you could—*(He indicates for* BILL *to take the tray from him.)*

BILL: *(Doing so)* Oh, righto.

GERALD: Thank you.

(GERALD *puts up the card table whilst* BILL *holds the tray.*)

Splendid. Now we can put that on here like so. *(Putting the tray on the table)* And I hereby declare the bar open. *(Looking enquiringly at* SUSAN) Dearest—?

SUSAN:   What I'd love more than anything else is a glass of Marsala.

GERALD:   It's your lucky day. *(He laughs.)* Bill?

BILL:   *(Joining in the joke)*—Er—I suppose you've got nothing in the house at all like—Marsala, have you? No?

GERALD:   No. Sorry. We've got Marsala if that's any good?

BILL:   Marsala? No, not heard of it. Never mind, I'll try that. *(Both men laugh.)*

SUSAN:   *(Under her breath)* Oh, my God. What did I start?

GERALD:   *(Never one to let a good joke go)* And I think—*(Deliberating)* Well, yes, I'll have the same. Why be different?

BILL:   Why indeed?

GERALD:   Good health, then.

BILL:   Good health.

SUSAN:   Cheers!

*(They drink.* SUSAN *and* BILL *react variously.* GERALD *seems happy with his drink.)*

BILL:   When did you last see your son, then?

GERALD:   Who, Rick? Oh, must be two years.

BILL:   Been away?

GERALD: Yes.

BILL: Abroad?

GERALD: No, no. Hemel Hempstead.

BILL: Ah. Working there, is he?

GERALD: No. He's—he's studying.

BILL: Right. What does he find to study in Hemel Hempstead, then?

GERALD: Er . . .

SUSAN: He belongs to this sect.

GERALD: No, it's not a sect, dear. It's a group. They prefer you to call them a group.

BILL: A religious order?

GERALD: Mmm. Mmm. Yes. Not I think strictly what one would term religious. Not in the conventional sense. Philosophical, perhaps, is nearer the mark.

SUSAN: Cranky.

GERALD: Now, now, Susan. We've agreed we mustn't prejudge.

SUSAN: I didn't and I have.

*(A slight pause.)*

BILL:   You'll be—looking forward to seeing him, no doubt.

GERALD:   Oh, yes. *(At his drink)* I think this is rather pleasant. It may be a bit sweet for you, dear, is it?

SUSAN:   It's lovely. *(She drains her glass and puts it down.)*

BILL:   If you want to chat to him, catch up on all his news, please don't worry about me. I'll be happy to sit and listen.

SUSAN:   I think I got that stuff for cooking. Years ago.

GERALD:   Ah.

BILL:   He'll probably want to chatter on, won't he? My two do. Whenever they're home. Can't get a word in.

GERALD:   Really? Well. It takes all sorts.

SUSAN:   The point is, Bill, our son doesn't talk to us at all.

BILL:   No?

GERALD:   Susan . . .

SUSAN:   Bill has to know, Gerald, if he's staying for lunch. Otherwise he'll wonder what on earth's going on. All of us miming to each other over the table.

GERALD:   I don't feel we necessarily need to share our little family problems with everyone . . .

SUSAN:   Little?

BILL:   Should I go? Would you rather I went?

GERALD:  *(Sharply)* No!

SUSAN:  *(Sharply)* No!

GERALD:  Please. Stay. It would, actually, be easier if you did, Bill. For us. So please. It's a phase we're both praying he'll grow out of—it's all to do with this group's somewhat over-emphatic reading of Matthew Chapter 10, I suspect. Verses 36 and 37. '. . . and a man's foes shall be they of his own household . . .' etcetera. Or again, Mark Chapter 3 verses 31 to 35—

SUSAN:  Yes, I think Bill's got the idea, Gerald . . .

BILL:  So he won't be speaking to you? At all?

GERALD:  No, probably not.

BILL:  Or listening to you? At all?

SUSAN:  No. We still keep his room for him. All his old things. His furniture. Equipment. Ridiculous.

BILL:  Yes, it hardly seems worth it, does it? Why is he bothering to come? If that's not a stupid question?

GERALD:  Well . . .

SUSAN:  No. Good question. Not to see us, certainly. Why is he coming, Gerald? Did he say in his letter?

GERALD:  He—er . . . *(To BILL)* He's allowed to write to us, you see—

SUSAN:  Gerald, why is he coming?

GERALD: He—he asked me . . . Well, he's in need of funds and he's—

SUSAN: He's getting nothing from us. Not for that lot.

GERALD: So he wants to sell all his personal possessions to raise money . . .

SUSAN: What personal possessions?

GERALD: His things. In his room. He wants to sell his room.

SUSAN: His room? He can't sell his room. You mean, the furniture?

GERALD: I think that's the idea . . .

SUSAN: *(Furiously)* You're going to let him sell his furniture? His desk? His bed? His swivel chair?

GERALD: Well, I can't see how—

SUSAN: I won't have it. You are not going to let him do that, Gerald. He can't sell them. They're things we gave him. They're our things. We gave them to him—

GERALD: No, dearest, they're *his* things. We gave them to *him*. That makes them *his*. You see?

SUSAN: *(Suddenly deeply distressed)* But . . . that's all that's left of him. If we sell . . . his bed . . . and his—swivel chair . . . then he'll have gone completely. We'll have nothing left of him at all.

GERALD: *(Touching her arm rather ineffectually)* I'm sorry, dear . . . I'm sorry . . .

SUSAN: I won't be able to sit in there, now. Like I do.

GERALD: No. But I don't see how we can . . .

*(They both stand miserably for a moment. BILL is appalled.)*

BILL: *(Making a move)* Look, I've just remembered, I've got a—

GERALD: Don't go, Bill. Please. We'd like you here. *(Trying to comfort SUSAN)* You know, it just occurred to me. Maybe he'll be allowed to talk to Muriel. She's not immediate family, is she? I don't know if they include aunts. We could try him with Muriel . . .

SUSAN: Who the hell would want to talk to Muriel?

GERALD: *(Lamely)* It might be worth a try . . .

BILL: What about—me? Would he talk to me?

GERALD: Oh, yes, he'll talk to you. No problem there.

BILL: In that case, if there's—anything you'd like me to ask him . . . for you—I'll . . .

GERALD: Thank you, Bill. Thank you. We may call on you.

*(A slight pause. SUSAN, who has grown listless after her outburst, has wandered away from them again, leaving her sherry glass on the card table. In the course of her wanderings, she comes across her glass of champagne and drinks it.)*

SUSAN:    *(Dully)* Cheers.

GERALD:    More Marsala, anyone?

BILL:    No, no. This is perfect.

GERALD:    I think I might. I think I could. Is this your glass, Susan? You'll join me, won't you? Yes. *(He pours them both another.)*

(MURIEL *comes on, hot and flustered, with a bowl of nuts.)*

Ah, Muriel. Everything in hand, is it?

MURIEL:    Everything's in hand. *(Putting bowl down)* Some nibbles. Susan, the herbs in the red tin by the tea pot? I couldn't be sure if they were thyme or sage.

SUSAN:    In the red tin?

MURIEL:    Yes.

SUSAN:    That's Earl Grey Tea.

MURIEL:    *(Worried)* Earl Grey Tea. Right. *(Moving off)* I do wish you'd label things, Susan. It's a very inconvenient kitchen to work in, it really is . . .

(MURIEL *goes.)*

GERALD:    Yes. Well. Good health.

SUSAN:    Cheers. *(She drains her Marsala.)*

GERALD:    Steady, dear . . .

(SUSAN *ignores him.*)

You've got children of course, haven't you, Bill?

BILL:   Yes. Katie and Caroline. Caroline I think's going to be the doctor. She's at Guy's. And Katie's just got a music scholarship to Cambridge.

SUSAN:   *(Miserably)* Lovely.

GERALD:   *(Unhappily)* Yes.

BILL:   *(Embarrassedly)* Both as thick as six bricks really. Like their parents. But they—seem to have muddled through. Somehow.

(MURIEL *hurries back.*)

MURIEL:   He's here. Ricky's here. I heard the front doorbell. I had a look. It's him.

GERALD:   Did you let him in?

MURIEL:   No, I—

GERALD:   Well, let him in, Muriel. We must let him in. Bill, I wonder if you'd mind—

BILL:   Do you want me to come?

GERALD:   If you would be so good. Just in case we need to communicate with each other . . .

BILL:   Surely.

GERALD:  Thank you so much.

MURIEL:  I hope he still likes omelettes . . .

(BILL *and* MURIEL *go.* GERALD *is on the point of following when he sees that* SUSAN *hasn't moved.*)

GERALD:  Susan, are you coming?

SUSAN:  In a moment . . .

GERALD:  He's arrived. Rick's here.

SUSAN:  *(Sharply)* In a minute, Gerald.

GERALD:  *(Flustered)* All right. All right.

(GERALD *goes.* SUSAN *hesitates and then reluctantly makes to follow. As she does so,* LUCY *reappears.*)

LUCY:  Mummy?

SUSAN:  *(Without looking at her)* Oh, hallo, darling.

LUCY:  Are you coming to eat? Everything's ready . . .

SUSAN:  I can't today, darling, I'm sorry—

LUCY:  *(Hurt)* What?

SUSAN:  I have to—have lunch somewhere else.

LUCY:  Somewhere else?

SUSAN:  Yes.

LUCY:  But what about us? What about the family? You can't leave us . . .

SUSAN:  *(Rather desperate)* I'm sorry. Another time . . .

(LUCY *stands shattered.* SUSAN *turns to go, aware of the effect she has had upon her daughter. She nearly collides with* GERALD *returning.)*

GERALD:  He's gone upstairs to his room. Bill says he says he'll be down in a minute . . .

SUSAN:  Have you seen Ricky yourself?

GERALD:  No. Not yet. Not personally. I heard him talking to Bill. I hid in the hall cupboard. Suddenly I lost my nerve and hid in the cupboard. Quite ridiculous. What if Rick had opened the door? What if he'd had a coat? Please come along, Susan. Please.

SUSAN:  Just give me a moment, Gerald.

GERALD:  I've given you ample moment, now come on.

(MURIEL *enters.)*

MURIEL:  Are you all coming to the table or not? Things are starting to burn, you know . . .

GERALD:  All right, all right. *(With a despairing glance back as he goes)* Please, Susan . . .

(GERALD *and* MURIEL *go out.* GERALD *taking the bottle and nuts with him.)*

SUSAN: *(Making to take a step)* God, I think I'm drunk.

(TONY *enters with a small garden table, already laid for four, which he sets down on the grass.*)

TONY: Andy says that if no one is coming in to lunch, then lunch must come to you. Come on, young Lucy, shift yourself and give us a hand.

LUCY: *(Brightening)* Right.

(LUCY *hurries off.*)

TONY: *(To* SUSAN) One moment, madam. The waitress is fetching you a chair.

SUSAN: No, I can't stop, Tony, I have to go . . .

TONY: What, with all that champagne to finish—?

SUSAN: Really . . .

(LUCY *re-enters with two chairs which she sets at the table.*)

TONY: There we are, you see. Allow me . . . *(He takes* SUSAN's *hand.*)

LUCY: Luncheon is served.

SUSAN: *(Pulling back)* No . . . No. Why won't you understand? Why won't you let me go inside?

TONY: *(Letting go of her hand)* The truth? Because we love you and we don't want to see you hurt. If you want the truth.

SUSAN: What are you talking about? What nonsense. No-body's going to hurt me.

LUCY: *(Sadly)* They will, Mummy. They always do. Admit it.

SUSAN: *(A moment's deliberation)* Very well, I'll eat with you.

*(She moves slowly to the table.)*

TONY: *(With a whoop)* I'll get the rest.

*(TONY goes off.)*

SUSAN: *(Brightening immediately as she surveys the table)* Oh, doesn't this look pretty!

LUCY: *(Indicating the chair facing away from the house)* Here, Mummy, you sit here. You must have the view of the lake.

*(SUSAN is about to sit as BILL enters.)*

BILL: *(Tentatively)* Susan, I . . .

LUCY: *(Passing SUSAN hissing)* Tell him to go away.

BILL: We were all wondering if you were coming in. We've all sat down, you see. And we were wondering if you were. Coming. In. Are you?

*(During this, TONY re-enters with two more chairs. LUCY has gone off momentarily.)*

TONY: Tell him to get lost.

SUSAN:   No, Bill, I'm not. I'm sorry. Can you explain to them I couldn't face being indoors, just at present?

BILL:   *(Lingering)* Yes. OK. It's just—

SUSAN:   *(Irritably)* What?

(LUCY *re-enters with three more champagne glasses and the bottle. During the next, she sets these, together with* SUSAN's *glass, on the table.*)

TONY:   *(Cheerfully)* Tell him take a jump . . .

BILL:   Well, if you could see it from . . .

LUCY:   Mind his own business . . .

BILL:   My point of view . . .

TONY:   Drop dead.

LUCY:   Drop dead.

BILL:   I mean, I'm nothing to do with any of this. I'm just stuck in the middle. I feel like an interpreter at some very, very hostile summit conference . . . Frankly, Susan, it's a very large price to pay for an omelette. So. Please.

SUSAN:   Oh, Bill, do drop dead.

BILL:   *(After a slight pause, crushed)* Fair enough.

(BILL *goes off.*)

TONY:   That's telling him.

LUCY: Nice one, Mummy . . . Now, do sit down.

TONY: Yes, sit down.

SUSAN: Yes.

(SUSAN *sits slowly, still rather shocked at what she has said to* BILL.)

I must be terribly drunk. That's the only excuse I have.

(ANDY *enters with a dish of elaborately garnished and decorated cold salmon.*)

ANDY: *(With a flourish)* Tarrah!

TONY: Oh, just take a look at that!

LUCY: Fabulous!

(LUCY *and* TONY *applaud as* ANDY *sets the dish down.* SUSAN *is still rather bewildered.*)

What do you think of that, Mother?

SUSAN: *(Faintly)* Wonderful. Thank you.

ANDY: There was an unkind rumour flying around my kitchen at one point that you were about to be tempted away from all this by a mere omelette. I trust that wasn't true?

SUSAN: No . . .

TONY: *(Filling their glasses)* False alarm.

LUCY:   All lies, Daddy . . .

ANDY:   I should hope so. I'd have been totally grief-stricken
for days . . . *(Raising his glass)* Well, here's to it, then. To
us all. The family.

ALL:   The family!

*(They toast each other.)*

ANDY:   I know what I wanted to ask. Have we heard any
news from Cambridge about your music scholarship,
Lucy?

LUCY:   Nope. Not a word, yet.

TONY:   She'll get it. She's brilliant.

ANDY:   Not if she doesn't practise, she won't—

LUCY:   I do practise.

ANDY:   Really? Have you seen the cello of yours lately,
young lady? It's got about three inches of dust on it. Mrs
Simmonds nearly hoovered it up twice . . .

*(They all laugh.* SUSAN *manages a smile, aware they're trying to
cheer her up.)*

LUCY:   *(Laughing)* Honestly, Daddy, that's a total exaggera-
tion. I practised on Tuesday—

TONY:   *(Shouting her down)* No, you didn't—

LUCY:   I did! And on Thursday . . .

ANDY: Not Thursday. You were out with me on Thursday . . .

LUCY: Only in the afternoon—

TONY: Rubbish! Rubbish! All rubbish!

*(As their voices reach a cacophonous peak, RICK enters unobtrusively from the direction of the house. He is in his early twenties. Contrary perhaps to expectations, there is nothing at all extraordinary or alarming about his appearance. He is dressed casually, suggesting a person with little or no interest in his personal appearance.)*

RICK: *(Softly)* Mum . . .

*(ANDY, who is facing that way, is the first to see RICK. He stops and stares. The others, noting ANDY's expression, follow suit. SUSAN is the last to turn.)*

Mum?

SUSAN: *(Stunned)* Rick?

*(She gets up, rather unsteadily. She stares at her son unbelievingly.)*

Ricky? Is that you? Speaking?

RICK: Yes. We wondered if you were coming in for lunch?

SUSAN: Oh, yes. Yes, of course . . .

*(She starts to make her way, somewhat uncertainly, towards the house. The family continue to stare.)*

RICK: Can you manage?

SUSAN: Yes. Oh, yes. *(She reaches the middle of the garden and sways.)* I wonder—I wonder if one of you would be so good as to hold on to me for a moment?

RICK: *(Moving to steady her)* Mum?

SUSAN: I just feel a little sleepy. I'll be fine in a—*(As her knees begin to buckle under her)* Oh, no . . . Here I go again . . .

*(As she falls, RICK catches her. We hear her long drawn-out cry. She sinks into a drink-induced oblivion, causing a blackout.)*

*End of Act One*

# ACT TWO

ACT TWO

*Darkness.*

*We hear the sound of* SUSAN's *groan as she comes out of her swoon. As she opens her eyes, the lights come up. It is a few seconds later. She is lying on the grass rather as at the start of the play, only this time* RICK *is bending over her.*

RICK: Mum?

(SUSAN *stares at him.*)

Mum?

SUSAN: *(Bemused)* Ricky?

*(She sits up with difficulty.)*

Ricky? I dreamt you spoke to me. Are you speaking to me? Is it you?

RICK: Yes, it's me. It's Rick speaking.

SUSAN: What's happened? *(Smiling)* It must be Mother's Day. Or have you got special dispensation?

RICK: No, I've left the group.

SUSAN: You have? When?

RICK: Oh—three months ago. Something like that.

SUSAN:  Why didn't you come and see us before?

RICK:  I had one or two things to sort out.

SUSAN:  Oh. I see. Well, I don't know what your reasons for leaving were, but I can't pretend that I'm not delighted at the news. If it means we'll be able to see you occasionally. Talk to you like a normal human being.

RICK:  *(Non-committally)* Yes.

SUSAN:  Where are you living now? Not still in Hemel Hempstead?

RICK:  No, I've moved back into London. South London.

SUSAN:  I see. And so? What are you doing? Have you got a job?

RICK:  Not just at present, no.

SUSAN:  Must be difficult, then? Making ends meet? Oh, this feels so odd talking to you—like a stranger. Do you have a room in South London?

RICK:  No, we've got a flat.

SUSAN:  We?

RICK:  Me and this girl.

SUSAN:  Oh? You've got a girl friend?

RICK:  Well, she's more than that, really.

SUSAN:  *(Smiling rather coyly)* A lover, then?

RICK:  No. Really, more of a wife, really . . .

SUSAN:  *(Blankly)* A wife?

RICK:  Yeah.

SUSAN:  You're married.

RICK:  Yeah.

SUSAN:  When? When did you marry?

RICK:  About two months ago. Tess, she was with the group, too and—we both decided we'd had enough really. I mean, we'd got what we could from it . . .

SUSAN:  Yes, yes . . .

RICK:  And we felt we'd grown, you know, through it.

SUSAN:  Yes. Good. Yes.

RICK:  So we left. And we thought maybe we should give things a week or two, you know, just to see them in perspective. You know?

SUSAN:  Yes.

RICK:  And—things seemed OK so we got married. You know.

SUSAN:  Where?

RICK:  Where?

SUSAN:  Where did you get married?

RICK:  Some registry office, I can't—

SUSAN:  Which one?

RICK:  *(Slightly irritably)* I don't know which one, Mum. It doesn't matter, does it?

SUSAN:  No, no. No. *(Slight pause.)* You didn't even tell us. Send us a—card.

RICK:  No.

SUSAN:  And you haven't brought her with you . . .

RICK:  No.

SUSAN:  Tess? That's her name?

RICK:  Yeah.

SUSAN:  Did you have to get married? Was she . . . ?

RICK:  No, of course she wasn't. We wouldn't have got married just because of that.

SUSAN:  Then why did you?

RICK:  Why does anybody? We love each other.

SUSAN:  Oh, yes. Of course. I just thought perhaps—

RICK: What?

SUSAN: You'd got married as another way to get back at us. Your father and me. Silly idea, is it?

RICK: It's a bloody ridiculous idea.

SUSAN: Yes. *(Sits with a little cry of grief)* Oh . . . Sorry. I'll be all right in a moment.

RICK: *(Muttering)* I knew you'd take it like this—

SUSAN: Well, what did you expect?

*(LUCY appears at a distance from them.)*

LUCY: *(Calling softly)* Mother . . . Mother . . .

SUSAN: Oh, do go away . . .

RICK: What?

SUSAN: Nothing.

*(LUCY, a little hurt, sits at some distance from them and watches unobtrusively.)*

SUSAN: You haven't told your father yet, I take it?

RICK: No.

SUSAN: What on earth's he going to say?

RICK: Quite a lot, probably. Not a man of few words when several spring to mind, is he?

SUSAN: *(Laughing)* Oh, that's very good, Ricky. Sums him up exactly. When I think what he and I could have achieved with our lives if he hadn't insisted on discussing everything first . . . *(Brightening)* Well, we must make up for lost time, mustn't we? The first thing is to meet Tess. Get to know her. You must both come and stay, that's what you must do.

RICK: No, the point is that Tess is a trained nurse, you know, and she's got this offer of a job. Overseas.

SUSAN: Overseas?

RICK: Yes. So we'll probably both be going pretty soon.

SUSAN: Where?

RICK: Thailand.

SUSAN: Thailand? *(Blankly)* That's miles.

RICK: Yes.

SUSAN: *(Distressed again)* Oh, Ricky . . . What are *you* going to do there? In Thailand? While she's—nursing?

RICK: I don't know. Help out, you know. Sort of odd job man, probably.

SUSAN: Do they have odd job men in Thailand?

RICK: They soon will do.

SUSAN:   So we aren't even going to meet this—Tess? Tess. Not a terribly attractive name, is it? Tess. A bit lumpen, isn't it? Are we going to see her or not?

RICK:   No. It's not possible this time round. I'll be staying a couple of days. I'm planning to sell off a few old things of mine. Raise a bit of spare cash. Then we're both off at the end of next week.

SUSAN:   Well, she could come down while you were here, couldn't she?

RICK:   No, she's got her own stuff to sort out, you see.

SUSAN:   She could come for the day? For lunch?

RICK:   I'd rather she didn't.

SUSAN:   You would?

RICK:   Yeah. I don't really want her coming here yet.

SUSAN:   Why? Because of your father? Well, we can keep him out of the way, can't we? They need hardly meet at all. Don't worry, I'll arrange things . . .

RICK:   It's only partly Dad.

SUSAN:   Well, who else? *(Slight pause.)* Me?

RICK:   Yeah. Just a bit. Sorry.

SUSAN:   You don't want me to meet her?

RICK:   No. Not yet. Maybe in a couple of years. We'll see.

SUSAN:  A couple of years? What am I supposed to do? Fly
out to Thailand for tea? Don't be ridiculous. Why can't I
meet her now?

RICK:  I can't go into it now, Mum. I'd just rather you didn't,
that's all.

SUSAN:  I feel I have a right to know why.

RICK:  Because—Tess is fairly—well . . . I suppose you'd
call her unsophisticated, in a way. And a bit shy. With
people.

SUSAN:  Gauche, I think, is the word you're looking for.

RICK:  No, not gauche. She looks at things simply, that's all.
She's straightforward. I just don't think she could cope
with you. Not with your attitude.

SUSAN:  What attitude?

RICK:  Well . . . I remember how you used to be with girls
I used to bring home.

SUSAN:  I remember, too. We got on terribly well.

RICK:  No, you didn't, Mum. I mean, frankly, you used to
embarrass the hell out of them. Didn't you know that?

SUSAN:  Nonsense.

RICK:  You did. You used to get them into corners and start
going on about—I don't know—contraception methods
and multiple orgasms . . . I mean, I'd hardly even kissed
them, you were asking them for their medical histories.

SUSAN: Nonsense, they were sixteen, seventeen-year-old girls who needed to know these things . . . I wasn't having a woman going out with a son of mine who didn't know what she was about. You'd have thanked me for it later . . . You? You didn't know a thing till I told you.

RICK: Yes, I did. We all did. It's just we didn't necessarily want to sit down and talk to you about it. I mean, if you started on like that with Tess she'd die.

SUSAN: All right, I won't.

RICK: You will.

SUSAN: I promise.

RICK: You will. Because you can't help it. You always want to finish up being girl friends with them, that's what it is.

SUSAN: Better than some mother-in-laws. Deadly rivals.

RICK: Maybe that's healthier.

SUSAN: Don't be so silly. Right. Your lecture is noted and understood. Thank you. All through your childhood I embarrassed the life out of you. Well, may I say from my side, Ricky, I think you are selfish, insensitive and priggish.

(RICK *doesn't reply.*)

Mention the word sex to you, you go pink round the ears. Just like your father. I presume that's the reason you buried yourself in Hemel Hempstead. Was it? With that bunch of cranks. To avoid me?

*(No reply.)*

Obviously, from that, I assume it was. Wonderful. So I've
been a total failure, have I? As a mother as well as a—

RICK: Nobody said that.

SUSAN: It's a shame you told me that. Up to now, I always
thought I'd managed rather well. I should have had a
daughter. I could have coped with her. *(Rather waspishly)*
Boys are all such delicate blossoms, aren't they?

(LUCY *looks up.*)

RICK: I don't want to hurt you any more, Mum, but God
help any daughter who had you as a mother.

*(A pause.)*

Look, don't take it all personally. It wasn't just you. There
was Dad as well. Looking them all up and down. Terrified
they'd turn out to be the daughters of Beelzebub. Scarlet
women after his son's body. Tess came straight to the
group from a convent education and training. She knows
all about the theory of life. Don't worry. But she's still a
bit short on the practical. And she needs to be introduced
to certain elements of it gradually. Elements like you and
Dad.

SUSAN: It's no use. You can be as loyal to your father as you
like. I know which one of us was really responsible for all
this . . .

RICK: *(Wearily)* Mum . . .

(GERALD *comes from the house.*)

GERALD:    Ah, you're here! We all wondered where you—*(He suppresses a burp.)*—wondered where you'd vanished off to. Bill's gone. I think the combination of potential family traumas and Muriel's cooking proved altogether too much for the poor man. *(Another suppressed burp.)* I beg your pardon. You know that really was quite the most appalling meal I've ever tasted. I'd forgotten how bad she was. Burnt Earl Grey omelettes. It's almost an art form to mistreat food in that way.

RICK:    How long's she staying?

GERALD:    Just until she—

SUSAN:    For ever.

GERALD:    —finds someone else to share her cooking, I suppose. Yes, probably for ever. Still, what are we to do? She's no huge problem. She spends most of her life trying vainly to contact her late husband, where's the harm?

(TONY *wanders on. He is dressed for the shoot. A twelve-bore shotgun (loaded but broken open) over his arm. An empty bag for game slung over his shoulder.* SUSAN *watches him.*)

You two been having a heart to heart? Have I missed anything? Any startling news?

SUSAN:    *(Looking at him, acidly)* Quite a bit, I'd say.

GERALD:    What's that dreadful look supposed to mean? Eh? If looks could kill . . . *(He laughs.)*

(SUSAN *looks away.*)

I take it there's some problem. Rick, is there a problem?

RICK:   I think I'll leave Mum to tell you, Dad. *(Going)* I must start sorting out my stuff . . .

GERALD:   Just as you wish, son. Just as you wish.

(RICK *goes off to the house.*)

*(Calling after him)* If you need the receipts for anything I probably still have them. *(More to himself)* Probably. Filed away.

SUSAN:   F for furniture. F for family.

GERALD:   Are you going to tell me, then? Rick's news?

SUSAN:   Yes, of course. What would you like to hear about first? His runaway registry office wedding? His wife? Mouselike Tess, the nervous nursing novice. His forthcoming trip to Thailand? His—

GERALD:   Just a minute. Just a minute. Thailand?

SUSAN:   Thailand. *(Waving vaguely)* It's over there . . .

TONY:   *(Helpfully indicating)* That way.

SUSAN:   That way. Somewhere. Past India.

GERALD:   *(Irritably)* Yes, I know where Thailand is. Why's he going there? As a missionary?

SUSAN: As an odd job man, so I understand.

GERALD: I don't quite follow all this. You say he has a wife?

SUSAN: A bride of two months.

GERALD: Why didn't he tell us?

SUSAN: I should have thought that was fairly obvious.

GERALD: Yes. I suppose so. All the same, I don't think it's fair to lay all the blame at your door . . .

TONY: What?

LUCY: What?

SUSAN: What?

GERALD: There are probably two sides.

LUCY: Mother, don't stand for this . . .

SUSAN: My door? Did I hear you correctly?

LUCY: Her door?

SUSAN: My door?

TONY: Want me to shoot him?

SUSAN: No.

GERALD: No, I'm saying, there are usually two sides—

SUSAN:  How dare you?

LUCY:  How dare he?

TONY:  Perfectly easy to shoot him . . .

SUSAN:  *(To* TONY) No. *(To* GERALD) How dare you stand there and—

GERALD:  Now, Susan, I'm not going to start on this. We have argued our lives away over that boy and we're not going to do it any more. I refuse to become involved—

SUSAN:  You smug—

LUCY:  Self-satisfied—

SUSAN:  Self-satisfied—

TONY:  Conceited—

SUSAN:  Conceited . . . bastard!

(LUCY *and* TONY *cheer and applaud this last effort of* SUSAN*'s.)*

GERALD:  *(Wagging a finger admonishingly)* Ah-ah-ah-ah! Ah-ah-ah-ah! Now. Now.

SUSAN:  *(Softer)* Bastard!

(MURIEL *comes on carrying a tray with four coffee cups.)*

MURIEL:  Here comes a lovely cup of coffee.

GERALD:  *(Startled)* What?

TONY:  Yurk. I'll see you later.

(TONY *goes off.*)

SUSAN:  No, thank you, Muriel.

GERALD:  Ah. No, no, no, no, Muriel. Thanks. Enough is as good as—enough. Thank you.

MURIEL:  No?

GERALD:  I must get back to my labours.

SUSAN:  That's right. Back to your bloody book.

MURIEL:  *(Shocked)* Now, now, now, Susan. That's no way to talk to him.

GERALD:  It's all right, Muriel. Susan is a little—*(He suppresses a burp.)*—she's just a little bit—*(Another burp.)*—would you excuse me, I've got the most terrible . . . Excuse me.

(GERALD *hurries off.*)

MURIEL:  *(Concerned)* Now look what you've done? Shouting at him like that. You've given him indigestion . . . The trouble with you is, Susan, you never learnt how to treat a man properly . . .

SUSAN:  *(Sarcastically)* I don't know what you know about these things, Muriel, I'm sure . . .

(MURIEL *goes off after* GERALD, *cluckingly concerned.*)

*(Yelling after her angrily)* Don't blame me. Blame your poi-

sonous omelettes . . . *(Muttering)* Everyone's blaming me. Everyone. For everything.

*(*LUCY *now moves closer to* SUSAN, *comfortingly.)*

LUCY:    Mother? . . . Mummy, don't be unhappy. *(Kneeling by* SUSAN*)* Can we talk about my wedding?

SUSAN:    *(Rather more curtly than normal)* Yes, we will do, darling, but not just at this moment.

LUCY:    Even if they don't appreciate you, we love you, Mother.

SUSAN:    Yes, thank you, darling.

LUCY:    I think you're just the most marvellous person—ever. Do you know what it said in the *Sunday Times* about you, last week? It said you were the most brilliant woman heart surgeon there was in this country. It said—

SUSAN:    *(Snapping)* Oh, do shut up, Lucy. For heaven's sake, don't be so stupid. I'm not a heart surgeon. I never have been. Now go away.

LUCY:    *(Hurt)* Yes, Mother.

*(Her eyes brimming with tears, she rises and rushes away.)*

SUSAN:    *(Immediately remorseful)* Oh, I'm sorry. I'm sorry. Come back. I'm sorry.

*(*GERALD *re-enters from the other direction.)*

GERALD:    *(As he does so)* All right. Apology accepted.

SUSAN:  I wasn't—

GERALD:  Mmmm?

SUSAN:  Nothing. What do you want?

GERALD:  I have returned for my card table. I need it in my
study for my pages. Oh, by the way, Mrs Ogle telephoned
me from next door. An operation which involved us both
in a great deal of shouting. She's apparently lost her dog.
Spike. You haven't seen Spike, have you? It hasn't got in
here?

SUSAN:  No.

GERALD:  Probably in the road. Under a truck. Right. (*He
makes to leave.*)

SUSAN:  Gerald . . .

GERALD:  (*Turning back*) Mmm?

SUSAN:  You don't feel we should perhaps talk.

GERALD:  No. I don't quite honestly. I don't at all. I think
talking has got us precisely nowhere. East is East. Never
the twain shall meet. Jack Spratt could eat no fat. We beg
to differ.

SUSAN:  You put everything so well, Gerald. No wonder
you're a writer.

GERALD:  I think I detect sarcasm. I can't be doing with sarcasm. You know what they say? Sarcasm is the greatest
weapon of the smallest mind. I'll see you at tea-time.

SUSAN:   If you leave me now for that damn—book, I warn you, Gerald, you will have nailed up the final—door—in our relationship . . .

GERALD:   Nailed up the final door? What is this nonsense? *(He turns and goes.)*

SUSAN:   You will have dug that final yard of moat between us!

GERALD:   *(In the distance)* Rubbish! Rubbish!

*(GERALD has gone.)*

SUSAN:   *(Still ploughing on)* You will have— You will have uncoiled the final strands of electrified barbed wire that serve to keep us—*(Giving up)* Oh, what's the use?

*(She is alone now. She stares at the sky and listens. The garden grows darker as though moving towards sunset. After a moment, ANDY appears and watches her. SUSAN does not look at him.)*

ANDY:   Beautiful, isn't it? The sunset?

SUSAN:   *(Without turning)* Yes, we're very lucky. Having all this.

ANDY:   *(Moving closer to her)* I hear you were angry with Lucy.

SUSAN:   I'm sorry. Did she tell you?

ANDY:   She only wanted to please you.

SUSAN:   I know, I know . . .

ANDY: Her whole world falls apart when you do that—

SUSAN: All right, Andy, don't keep on at me. I'm sorry.

ANDY: *(Kissing the back of her neck)* Forgiven.

SUSAN: *(Wriggling with pleasure)* Mmmm. How do you make me feel so helpless? You only have to touch me and my knees give way . . .

(ANDY *laughs.* TONY *strolls into view, returning from his shoot. His bloodstained game bag now contains something freshly killed.)*

TONY: Hi! It's a lovely evening for doing whatever it is you look as if you're both thinking of doing . . .

ANDY: On your way, callow youth. Any luck?

TONY: Just the one. *(He holds up the bag.)*

ANDY: Well, better than nothing.

SUSAN: What is it? What have you shot?

TONY: Nothing, old love. Just a rodent.

SUSAN: What sort of rodent?

TONY: *(Shrugging)* A rodent's a rodent, isn't it?

SUSAN: I want to see.

TONY: *(Wandering off)* I'll show you later . . .

ANDY: He'll show you later.

TONY:   Once it's skinned and cooked . . . See you.

(TONY *wanders off.*)

SUSAN:   Andy, what has he just killed?

ANDY:   Oh, darling, how should I know? He shoots anything that moves. You know Tony.

SUSAN:   (*Drawing back from him a little*) No, I don't think I do know Tony. Not any more. Any more than I think I know you. You've altered. You've all altered, recently.

ANDY:   Darling . . . Come on.

SUSAN:   What do you want from me? What are you doing here?

ANDY:   You know that . . .

SUSAN:   No, I don't. What?

ANDY:   We're here because you asked us here.

SUSAN:   No. That's just the point, you see. That was how it was, originally. Yes. I whistled and you came. Yes. But not now. You just keep popping up. All of you. That girl. She's taken to just coming and sitting there, now, staring at me for ages on end—

ANDY:   That girl's your daughter.

SUSAN:   Well, whoever. I was having a private conversation. Why was she sitting there?

ANDY:  She felt you needed her.

SUSAN:  Well, I didn't. I was perfectly able to cope. And now Tony's started. Chipping in when I'm talking to someone.

ANDY:  If you don't want them, tell them to go away. They'll go. You've only to tell us. Any of us.

SUSAN:  Well, I am. I'm telling you now. Please go.

(ANDY *doesn't move.*)

Go on. Shoo. Vanish.

*(He smiles at her but still doesn't move.)*

There you are, you see. You don't take a blind bit of notice of me, do you? I've told you to go. You're still here.

ANDY:  Perhaps you didn't really mean it?

SUSAN:  Of course I meant it. I want to see Gerald now. Go away. I'm going to have a chat with Gerald about his book. It's absolutely riveting, you know. It's all about the parish since 1386. Did you know that until 1874 there used to be sheep grazing where the town hall is now? I bet you didn't know that. Or I might just pop upstairs and embarrass my son and discuss sexually transmitted diseases with him. Or help Muriel make a soap flake soup. *(Desperately)* What do you want from me? Just tell me. What do you all want?

ANDY:  Or—put another way . . .

SUSAN:  What other way?

ANDY:   There is no—

SUSAN:   There is no—

ANDY:   —other way to—

SUSAN:   —other way to—

ANDY:   —why are you—

SUSAN:   —why are you—

ANDY:   —saying everything—

SUSAN:   —saying everything—

ANDY:   —before I do?

SUSAN:   —before I do?

ANDY:   Oh!

SUSAN:   *(With an angry cry of frustration)* Oh!

ANDY:   Or put another way—why are you repeating everything I say?

(SUSAN *opens and closes her mouth but decides not to speak.*)

Go on, say it. *(Prompting her)* Oh, God! What's happening to me?

SUSAN:   *(With a wail)* Oh, God! What's happening to me?

ANDY:   There are all sorts of games we can play, you see. With our minds.

SUSAN:  Go away. Please, go away.

ANDY:   *(Teasing)* Ah, now wait. Is that you telling me to go away or could that be me telling you to go away? It's sometimes hard to tell, isn't it?

SUSAN:  Please . . .

ANDY:   *(Adopting her tone)* Andy, I'm warning you . . .

SUSAN:  *(Adopting his tone)* Warning me of what exactly, Susie?

ANDY:   *(As SUSAN)* That if you don't . . . if you don't leave me . . . alone . . . Andy?

SUSAN:  *(As ANDY)* Anything wrong, Susie?

ANDY:   *(As SUSAN)* Oh, God! Where am I? Where have I gone?

SUSAN:  *(As ANDY)* You're over here.

ANDY:   *(As SUSAN)* No, I'm not. I'm over here . . .

SUSAN:  *(As TONY)* Where?

ANDY:   *(As SUSAN)* Who's that? Is that you, Lucy?

SUSAN:  *(As TONY)* No, this is Tony.

ANDY:   *(As SUSAN)* Andy! Andy!

SUSAN:   *(As* LUCY*)* Daddy? I'm here.

ANDY:   *(As* TONY*)* Hi! Big Sis?

SUSAN:   *(As* LUCY*)* Mummy! Where are you? I'm frightened.

ANDY:   *(As* SUSAN*)* I'm here, darling, I'm here.

SUSAN:   *(As* SUSAN*)* No, I'm here. *(As* LUCY*)* Mummy? *(As* SU-SAN*)* No, there.

ANDY:   *(As* LUCY*)* Mummy?

SUSAN:   *(As* SUSAN*)* No, everywhere. *(As* LUCY*)* Mummy? *(As* SUSAN*)* Oh God, I'm everywhere. What am I doing everywhere . . . It's like not . . . *(Slowly)* . . . Not being— anywhere. Where am I? Where am I now?

ANDY:   *(As* TONY*)* It's all right, Susie, you're there.

SUSAN:   I'm here?

ANDY:   Home where you belong.

SUSAN:   *(Staring at him in horror)* Who are you? Really?

(ANDY *smiles.)*

Oh, no. You go away. You keep away from me.

ANDY:   *(Laughing)* Beware, Susie! Nothing is who it is! No one is what he seems!

*(He goes. The sunset is replaced by a normal mild afternoon light.* SUSAN *looks about her apprehensively.)*

SUSAN: *(To herself, pleased)* They've gone. They have. They've all gone. Good. *(Shouting)* Don't come back, any of you. Ever. I don't want you, do you hear? Go away and stay away for ever.

*(BILL has entered unobtrusively behind her.)*

BILL: *(Cheerily)* Hallo. Does that include me?

*(SUSAN jumps with a stifled scream.)*

Sorry.

SUSAN: Oh, Bill. How glad I am to see you.

BILL: Really?

SUSAN: Really. You're just the person I need. Someone calm and unflappable and *sane* . . .

BILL: Thanks very much. I don't think I've ever been called that before. Well, not all three in the same breath, anyway . . .

SUSAN: I thought you'd left after lunch.

BILL: Yes, I did. I'm sorry. It was just there was some talk of a dessert and I'm afraid I lost my nerve. Then halfway home I thought, this won't do. What about you? What about my patient? So I'm back. Because, frankly, I'm still a fraction concerned about you, if you must know. You still seem a mite keyed up. Oh—*(Fumbling in his pocket)*—and I brought you these—*(He produces a bottle of pills.)*—which I already had. They might do the trick. They're fairly mild but if you can't sleep they may help. OK?

SUSAN:   May I ask you a question?

BILL:   I know what you're going to ask. Not more than four over 24 hours.

SUSAN:   No, that wasn't what I was going to ask—

BILL:   Ah. Wrong again. Yes?

SUSAN:   It's this. *(She hesitates.)* Well . . . Difficult to put without sounding absurd but . . . Do you believe that in this day and age it's possible for someone to be possessed?

BILL:   Possessed?

SUSAN:   Yes.

BILL:   You mean by demons? That sort of thing?

SUSAN:   That sort of thing.

BILL:   That's a—that's a bit out of my league, really. I mean, I'm not ducking the question—well, yes, I am ducking the question but— Why don't you ask Gerald? He's our man on the spot, surely?

SUSAN:   No, I don't want to ask Gerald. I'm asking you.

BILL:   *(Deliberating)* Well. The answer to that is . . . My answer to that is—like most of my answers to important questions, I'm afraid—is possibly, but I don't really know. It's a bit like—what?— 'Is there life on other planets?' The scientists say, Look here, we've just discovered X billion billion stars, Y billion billion of which certainly have planetary systems. And of these, Z billion billion have almost certainly got earth-type atmospheres, probably supporting life as we know it. So you look up at the sky and what do you see? Bugger all. Pardon the language. I mean according to those chaps, the sky up there should look like a beach at Bank Holiday. Absolutely teeming with little men dashing hither and thither. And instead, absolutely empty. But that's not to say scientists are wrong. But they could be. Sorry. So getting back to you. The answer's possibly. Why do you ask?

SUSAN:   It's just that I think I might be.

BILL:   You? Possessed?

SUSAN:   It's possible.

BILL:   Good Lord. Truly?

SUSAN:   You know I told you that I had these hallucinations a while back?

BILL:   You mean yesterday?

SUSAN:   Yesterday? Was it yesterday—? Well, the thing is, they haven't gone. I said they had but they haven't. They're still with me. Only more frequently.

BILL:   I see. I see. (He ponders.) Do they—er—do they happen at any particular time? Of the day? Of the month? After meals, say?

SUSAN:   (Rather coolly) I don't think they're a result of an upset stomach if that's what you're asking.

BILL: No, no. Fair enough. Just a shot in the dark. Sometimes these . . . You don't drink that much alcohol, do you?

SUSAN: *(Cooler still)* No.

BILL: Not on any sort of drugs, are you?

SUSAN: Only what you've just given me.

BILL: Yes. Well. You'll have your work cut out to hallucinate on those. No, it seems to me it's either our old friend the garden rake. Or . . .

SUSAN: Or?

BILL: It really is something you ought to talk to Gerald about.

SUSAN: I couldn't talk to Gerald. Not possibly—

BILL: If not as a vicar, at least as your husband.

SUSAN: That would be even worse. It would be like—undressing in front of him. *You* must understand, surely? Isn't it the case that some doctors' wives prefer not to consult their own husbands? Isn't that true?

BILL: Oh yes, quite common. Nora doesn't use me. She always goes to my partner, Geoff Burgess. Quite frequently, actually. I mean, she always looks perfectly fit to me, blooming. But she keeps finding all sorts of things wrong with her. Still . . .

SUSAN: Yes. Reverting to me, if we could . . .

BILL: I'm sorry. That's my problem, you see. I think as a doctor I'm perfectly sound, it's just that—

SUSAN: *(Interrupting)* It's just that the only alternative to all this, Bill, is that I'm going off my head . . .

BILL: Oh. No, no. Lord, no . . .

SUSAN: Are you sure?

BILL: Absolutely, positive. Listen, I've seen countless people going off their heads on several occasions and they were nothing like you . . . You're perfectly fine. Probably a bit run down, that's all.

SUSAN: Seeing things that nobody else sees? Are those the symptoms of someone who's just a bit run down?

BILL: Possibly, possibly . . .

SUSAN: Holding conversations with people who might not be there?

BILL: Yes, it's all—theoretically feasible . . .

SUSAN: *(Agitated)* If only somebody else saw them. Then I'd know I was sane—

BILL: Quite.

SUSAN: But nobody else is going to, are they? Because they're all in my head.

*(She paces about in a feverish manner. BILL watches her with increasing anxiety.)*

I know . . . that somehow . . . like those genies that live
in bottles, you know . . . If I can only keep them from
getting out . . . I'll be all right. They mustn't get out . . .
Whatever happens . . .

BILL:   Do you think that's wise . . . ?

SUSAN:   Why not?

BILL:   Well, surely, don't you feel that these—whatever they
are—are merely a symptom of something else?

SUSAN:   They are?

BILL:   Almost certainly. And with any symptom—I'm not a
psychiatrist—but with any medical symptom, it can be a
dangerous thing to suppress it. Or try and ignore it. A
symptom is simply something trying to signal. Something.
Put very simply. Try to suppress it and you're putting
your thumb over the valve of a pressure cooker.

SUSAN:   Yes, yes . . .

BILL:   *(Gaining in confidence as his theory takes shape)* At worst,
there'll be an almighty explosion and a great deal of dam-
age. Even at best, you're liable to finish up with your din-
ner all over the ceiling.

SUSAN:   It's wrong to bottle things up, then?

BILL:   Dangerous.

SUSAN:   But if let them out, these people, I don't know that I
can control them. Not any more.

BILL: Don't worry, Susan. I'm going to fix an appointment with someone for you. I know a good, reliable chap. And we'll fight it. If necessary we'll fight them off together.

SUSAN: *(Touched by his concern)* Oh, Bill . . . How can you fight something you can't see? It's up to me.

BILL: I can help.

SUSAN: If you could see them you could.

BILL: If I could, would it help?

SUSAN: Oh, yes. Of course it would.

*(A pause. BILL looks around.)*

BILL: They're—are they here at the moment?

SUSAN: No.

BILL: No? Oh, good. *(With a relieved laugh)* I was going to say, if they are here, I can't see them.

*(A pause. MURIEL comes on from the house, whistling rather feebly. They stare at her.)*

MURIEL: Spikey! You haven't seen him, have you?

BILL: Sorry?

MURIEL: Mrs Ogle's little Spike? She's lost him.

SUSAN: *(Rather guiltily)* Has she?

MURIEL: Funny. He usually comes if you whistle him. Must have run off . . . What a cup of tea, either of you?

BILL: *(Hastily)* No, thank you.

SUSAN: *(Equally hastily)* No, thanks.

MURIEL: Really? You sure?

SUSAN: *(Nastily)* You can make one for Gerald. He'd love one.

MURIEL: I'm going to. Spikey! Spikey!

*(MURIEL goes off whistling.)*

BILL: Tea. That was a near thing. *(He laughs.)*

*(SUSAN laughs with him. BILL feels encouraged.)*

Your son seems very nice.

SUSAN: Ricky? Oh, yes.

BILL: *(Laughing)* Not as bad as you feared, then? I presume?

SUSAN: No, no. Thankfully.

BILL: Left that place he was at?

SUSAN: Yes.

BILL: And what's he going to do now?

SUSAN:  Well . . . He's just told us some wonderful news, actually. We were very thrilled.

BILL:  Oh, what's that?

SUSAN:  He's getting married.

BILL:  Oh, super. Presentable, is she?

SUSAN:  How do you mean?

BILL:  The girl he's going to marry? That's always the big hurdle, isn't it? Who are they going to lumber you with as an in-law? Our two girls, they've both gone and settled for these awful whizz-kid stockbrokers. Dreadful wheeler-dealers with their hair curling over their ears. Socialists with Swiss bank accounts, you know the sort. Boring as hell. How's your daughter-in-law-to-be, then?

SUSAN:  She's—all right. Not striking, you know. Quite plain, but . . .

BILL:  Ah.

SUSAN:  Got one of those heavy faces. Bit jowly. Or it will be, when she's forty.

BILL:  Uh-huh.

SUSAN:  And that terribly fine hair that you can never quite do anything with. You just want to grab hold of it and cut it all off. Poor girl.

BILL:  *(Sympathetically)* Yes. Yes.

SUSAN:  Quite a thickset build—

BILL:  Well, so long as she's nice . . .

SUSAN:  Oh, yes. She's a dormouse.

BILL:  Are they moving in locally?

SUSAN:  No. They're off to the Far East, actually.

BILL:  That sounds exciting. How come?

SUSAN:  Well—Ricky has a job lined up there.

BILL:  Marvellous.

SUSAN:  And she's a Thai, actually.

BILL:  Yes, well, they can be, can't they?

SUSAN:  No, she's from Thailand. A Thai.

BILL:  Oh, heavens. Sorry. Yes.

SUSAN:  But as I say she's hardly that sparkling.

BILL:  Perhaps it's when she's with you. Maybe she feels a little bit outshone?

SUSAN:  (Modestly) Oh . . .

BILL:  I don't know. You do tend to—I don't know.

SUSAN:  What?

BILL: Well—linger on in the memory. You know.

SUSAN: Oh, really . . .

BILL: Yes, you do. It's a good job I'm not your regular doctor, isn't it? Otherwise that'd sound rather unethical.

SUSAN: Don't be so silly.

BILL: No, I do. I find you very attractive. And I have done for a very long time.

SUSAN: You only met me—when was it?—yesterday.

BILL: We've met before that.

SUSAN: Occasionally.

BILL: Quite occasionally. We never spoke to each other much, but I used to watch you. Talking to other people.

SUSAN: Did you?

BILL: Oh, yes.

SUSAN: When?

BILL: Oh, you know. At social things. Like—well, I remember the school concerts, particularly.

SUSAN: School concerts?

BILL: At Bilbury Lodge. You remember. All our kids leaping about in woolly animal ears, singing dreadful songs . . .

SUSAN: That was ten years ago.

BILL: Eleven. I know. Years.

SUSAN: Well. Honestly.

BILL: Sorry. I should never have told you, should I?

SUSAN: No.

BILL: I'm sorry.

SUSAN: I'm glad you did though. *(She smiles.)*

(BILL *smiles back. He looks at her and decides whether or not to kiss her. As he moves in gently, behind him,* LUCY *wanders on. She watches.* SUSAN, *naturally, sees her. She places her hand on* BILL'S *shoulder to stop him.)*

*(Softly)* Bill!

BILL: What?

SUSAN: She's here now. One of them's here now.

BILL: You mean one of your—

SUSAN: Yes. She's over there.

BILL: *(Turning cautiously)* Oh, yes?

SUSAN: Can you see her . . . ? Please God, you can see her — Can you see anything?

BILL: *(Try as he might)* Not . . . immediately.

SUSAN: If only you could see her, everything would be all right. I know it. *(Pointing)* She's there. She's just there.

LUCY: Mother?

SUSAN: There. That's my daughter. That's Lucy.

BILL: *(Staring at the spot where* SUSAN*'s pointing)* Lucy.

SUSAN: Do you see?

BILL: Keep describing her.

SUSAN: She's—quite tall. She's wearing a light-coloured dress and she's barefoot. Fair hair . . .

BILL: Hang on. Yes, yes. I see her.

SUSAN: You do? Kneeling down . . .

BILL: Yes, kneeling down. She's very pretty.

SUSAN: Oh, yes . . .

(BILL *moves towards* LUCY. *Though he can't see her, he makes a good stab at pretending he can. He crouches slightly to one side of* LUCY *and talks to the air.*)

BILL: *(Quite avuncular)* Hallo, there. You're a big girl, aren't you? How old are you, then?

(LUCY *stares at him mystified.*)

Bless my soul! Is that all? You look older than that. You must have been eating a lot of green vegetables.

LUCY:    *(Getting up)* Mother?

BILL:    They make you grow big and strong, did you know that? Did your Mummy ever tell you that? I bet she did.

LUCY:    *(Moving to* SUSAN *and leaving* BILL *happily chattering away)* Mother, who is he? What does he want?

SUSAN:    Nothing, darling. You're not to worry. He's just someone who—sees things . . .

LUCY:    How extraordinary. Is he mad?

SUSAN:    Possibly. One of us is anyway. And I'd sooner it were him.

LUCY:    Well, it certainly isn't you. Tell him to go away. He's untidying our beautiful garden.

(BILL *has been pretending to listen to his version of* LUCY. *He now responds to something she has said. Under the next, he keeps up a background conversation performing a conjuring trick with his pocket handkerchief to amuse her.)*

BILL:    *(Under the next)* Do you like spinach? Oh, you must eat your spinach. All little girls should eat up their spinach. And their lettuce. Do you eat your lettuce? Are you like a rabbit? Rabbits like lettuce, did you know that? Have you seen a rabbit round here? Wait a minute! Just a minute! I believe I have . . . *(Fumbling in his pocket)* . . . yes, I do have—a rabbit in my pocket. *(He produces his handkerchief with a flourish.)* Hey presto! What do you mean, this isn't a rabbit? Of course it's a rabbit. Wait! Wait! I'll show you. You see, we knot this . . . like this and then . . . this

. . . like this and— Look! There's a rabbit. Bo! Where's he gone now? Bo! etc. etc.

(TONY *enters and stares at* BILL *suspiciously.*)

TONY: What's that chap doing here?

LUCY: Mother says he's a madman. Tell him to go away, Tony.

TONY: Want me to chuck him out, Big Sis?

SUSAN: No, don't. He's not doing any harm, really.

TONY: What's he doing? Who's he talking to?

LUCY: He's so ugly, Mummy. He's so terribly ugly.

SUSAN: No, now you really mustn't call him that. He's been saying very sweet things to me . . .

TONY: *(His eyes narrowing)* Sweet things? What sort of sweet things?

SUSAN: Oh, just nice flattering things. Loving things.

LUCY: *(Scandalized)* How dare he?

TONY: Right. That settles it, I'm going to shoot him . . .

LUCY: Oh, good!

SUSAN: No, no!

(BILL *carries on blissfully unaware of the danger he is in.* ANDY *enters at this point and surveys the scene.*)

*(Running to him)* Andy, stop them. Do stop them. They're behaving most terribly badly.

ANDY:     What's going on, kids?

LUCY:     Daddy, that man's been saying awful, filthy things to Mummy. You must get rid of him . . .

TONY:     *(Simultaneously with her)* Look, I'll go and fetch the twelve-bore. It won't take a second . . .

SUSAN:    *(Simultaneously with both of them)* Don't listen to either of them. They're such liars both of them . . .

ANDY:     *(Quietening them)* All right, all right, all right! One at a time. First of all, who is he? Second, what's he doing?

LUCY:     He's mad, that's all . . .

ANDY:     Sssh! Susie, what's he doing here?

SUSAN:    Well, he was just—passing through . . .

TONY:     How can he be just passing through? It's a ten-mile walk to the main gate . . .

LUCY:     He was saying sweet things to Mother. She said so herself.

ANDY:     Susie, are they telling the truth? Why are you protecting him? Is it true?

SUSAN:  I—I can't answer.

ANDY:  Then I'll ask him. *(Calling across to* BILL*)* Hey, you!

SUSAN:  You can't ask him. He won't hear you . . .

*(She tails away as* BILL *turns, puzzled, and stares at them. The skies grow noticeably darker as he does so.)*

ANDY:  Yes, you. I'm talking to you. What are you doing here?

BILL:  Oh, hallo. Were you talking to me?

SUSAN:  *(With a wail, at this new turn of events)* Oh, my God . . . Now what's happening?

ANDY:  Have you been threatening my wife?

BILL:  Me? Good Lord, no.

TONY:  Who are you? Who were you talking to?

BILL:  Me? I'm a stockbroker and whizz-kid wheeler-dealer and I was trying to remember a poem.

LUCY:  A likely story. Punch him, Daddy.

SUSAN:  No, Andy . . .

BILL:  *(Alarmed)* Just a tick—

TONY:  *(Advancing menacingly)* If there's one thing I loathe and detest it's stockbrokers. What have you got in that case?

BILL: Nothing, nothing . . .

SUSAN: Don't hurt him!

LUCY: *(Jumping up and down)* Rabbits. He's got rabbits in that case. Our rabbits.

BILL: No, I haven't.

TONY: Have you got some of our rabbits in your case?

BILL: Of course not.

LUCY: Yes, he has. I heard him talking to them.

TONY: *(Swooping and grabbing the case with great speed)* Let's take a look, then.

BILL: Hey no, you can't have that. No . . .

SUSAN: Stop it! Stop it!

TONY: *(Tossing the case to* LUCY *who catches it)* Take a look, Lucy.

(LUCY *starts to open the case.* BILL *hops about trying to retrieve it from her but* TONY *blocks his path.* SUSAN *moves forward to assist* BILL *but is restrained gently but firmly by* ANDY.)

BILL: Look, you mustn't . . . You won't be able to open it anyway, it's jammed.

LUCY: What have we in here . . . ?

TONY: *(To* BILL) All right, take it easy. Take it easy.

SUSAN:  Bill . . . Andy, please—

ANDY:  It's all right, Susie. Leave it to them.

SUSAN:  But they mustn't touch his case, it's—

ANDY:  No, darling. He may be a poacher. If he's a poacher then we'll have to hang him.

SUSAN:  Hang him?

BILL:  What's that about hanging?

(LUCY *opens the case. It contains just one item. She drops the case and holds up a long garment which appears to have been made entirely of knotted string.*)

LUCY:  *(With a cry of glee)* Look what I've found! It's a dress. It's a lovely macramé dress. Thank you very much.

BILL:  No, no. That's not for you. Put that back. That's my daughter's—for her school concert. Put it back, I say . . .

LUCY:  *(Rushing off)* I can't wait to try it on . . .

(LUCY *goes off.* BILL *snatches up his discarded briefcase and follows her.*)

BILL:  Please don't. Please be careful. It isn't finished. There's another six week's work . . .

(BILL *goes off after her.* TONY *makes to follow.*)

TONY:  *(To* ANDY*)* What do you want me to do with him?

ANDY: *(With a glance at* SUSAN) Oh, just chuck him in the lake for the time being.

SUSAN: Oh, Bill . . .

ANDY: *(After the departing* TONY) Gently, Tony. Do it gently.

TONY: *(As he goes)* Righty-ho . . .

(TONY *goes off. It is now sunset again, as in the earlier scene when* ANDY *and* SUSAN *were alone together.)*

SUSAN: Oh, they're both so naughty.

ANDY: Don't be too hard on them, Susie.

SUSAN: Tony you expect it from. But Lucy . . .

ANDY: Well . . . You have to make allowances for a girl. After all, the night before her wedding. She's bound to be a bit overexcited, isn't she?

SUSAN: Yes, of course . . .

ANDY: Remember our wedding day?

SUSAN: What a question . . .

ANDY: We must try and make Lucy's day just as wonderful.

SUSAN: Nothing could ever be like ours. Remember our honeymoon? Remember Portugal?

ANDY: I do.

SUSAN:   And our first house? How poor we were, then.

ANDY:   I had to sell my desk and my swivel chair, so we
could eat . . .

*(They laugh.)*

SUSAN:   Eat? What about that first meal I cooked for us? In
the pressure cooker?

ANDY:   Best meal I've ever eaten off the ceiling.

*(They laugh again.)*

SUSAN:   You've never let me live that down. Not after—what
is it?—ten years.

ANDY:   Eleven. You're still as young. You haven't changed.
Just the same.

SUSAN:   Will Lucy's husband like me?

ANDY:   He will adore you. She will be wild with jealousy,
mark my words. *(Moving to her)* and if you reciprocate in
the slightest way, so will I be.

*(He kisses her softly. They sink to the ground.)*

SUSAN:   *(Murmuring)* Oh, Andy . . .

*(ANDY kisses her again, fleetingly.)*

ANDY:   Shhh!

*(He gently lies her back on the grass. He starts to kiss her neck. As he does so, SUSAN opens her eyes in brief horror, suddenly aware of her predicament.)*

SUSAN:   *(As he continues kissing her, softly)* Oh, dear God! I'm making love with the Devil . . .

*(She closes her eyes and surrenders to the happily inevitable. Simultaneously there is a blackout.*
*Then a tremendous clap of thunder. A short pause while it dies, then rain, a further rumble and a flash of lightning. SUSAN is revealed in the same place as before, on the grass, sprawled out, eyes now open, a smile on her face. Rain is pouring down on her. ANDY has gone. The dress SUSAN was wearing before has been loosened, perhaps unbelted at the waist to suggest that she is now in a nightdress. She has also shed her shoes.)*

GERALD:   *(Off, distant)* Susan! Susan! Where are you?

*(SUSAN half-registers this, but doesn't move. In a moment, from the direction of the house, GERALD's torch is seen bobbing into view. When he appears, we see he is dressed in dressing gown and slippers over his pyjamas.)*

*(Appearing)* Susan! Where have you gone? Su—?

*(He stops short as the torch beam falls upon SUSAN lying on the grass.)*

Susan? What on earth's happened to you? Susan?

SUSAN:   *(Dreamily)* Mmmm?

GERALD: *(Calling back behind him)* It's all right, she's here. She's out here. Lying in the middle of the lawn. *(Returning to her)* Susan, can you hear me?

SUSAN: Hallo, Gerald. How are things?

GERALD: *(Angrier now)* What on earth do you think you're playing at, woman? Lying out here on the grass at half past three in the morning? In the middle of a thunderstorm? Is this some sort of a joke?

SUSAN: Yes. Terribly funny, isn't it?

GERALD: No, it is not funny, Susan. It is not funny at all. Now please get up and come indoors. Up! Up!

SUSAN: Nope! Nope!

GERALD: *(Really angry)* Susan! Come along.

*(He seizes one of her hands and attempts to pull her to her feet or even, possibly, along the ground.)*

Hup . . . hup . . . oh . . .

*(He gives up the struggle. It is more difficult than he thought.)*

*(Rather breathless now)* Susan, I'm warning you, I shall— *(Turning and calling)* Rick! Rick! Come here! Give me a hand quickly, please! *(Returning to* SUSAN *again)* Susan, what has come over you? What on earth is the matter?

SUSAN: I'm fine. Fine. You mustn't worry, Gerald, you really mustn't . . .

GERALD:  *(Calling)* Rick!

SUSAN:  We'll get a nice quiet divorce.

GERALD:  *(Very startled)* Divorce?

SUSAN:  I promise I won't let it affect your career. I promise.

GERALD:  What?

SUSAN:  I won't make a scandal for you. I don't want to hurt you, really. I won't mention names, if you won't . . .

GERALD:  *(Furious)* What are you talking about? What on earth are you talking about? My dressing gown is wringing wet, my bedroom slippers are full of rainwater and I haven't the faintest idea what you're talking about. *(Yelling)* Rick! Where the—blazes is that boy? Oh, yes. Well, if you want to know where he is, I'll tell you where he is. He's putting out the fire, that's where he is.

SUSAN:  Fire?

GERALD:  The fire that mercifully woke me up before we fried in our beds. The fire in my study, presumably started by you . . .

SUSAN:  Me? Never . . .

GERALD:  Don't try and deny it, Susan.

SUSAN:  I've been out here.

GERALD:  All sixty pages blazing away. Do you realize the years of work that went into that book? The research? The background reading? The hours of grubbing around, rubbing tombstones? I was on my final chapter, Susan. How could you do it? 'And finally, what lessons are there to be learnt from the past 600 years of parish history? For is it not the duty of the present to learn from the past in order to prepare for the—' Oh, God!

*(A clap of thunder.)*

Forgive me for my feelings towards you at this moment, Susan. For they are unspeakable. Please come inside. I will forgive you in the dry.

SUSAN:   No, no. Don't worry about me. Go and look after your book, I'm all right . . .

(RICK *comes out from the house. He is dressed in similar fashion to* GERALD. *He holds one charred sheet of manuscript.*)

RICK:   Sorry, Dad, I did my—(*Seeing* SUSAN) Mum? What's the matter with Mum?

GERALD:   Did you manage to save any of it, Rick?

RICK:   What's the matter with Mum? What's she doing out here?

GERALD:   Never mind her. Did you manage to save any of my book?

RICK:   Well, yes. That. That's all.

GERALD:   (*Snatching it from him and shining his torch on it*) Page 57. (*Brandishing the page at* SUSAN) That's it. That's what's left. Are you satisfied, woman?

SUSAN: It wasn't me . . .

GERALD: *(Dropping to his knees on the grass)* Why, Susan, why?

SUSAN: . . . I've been out here.

GERALD: Why? What terrible, nameless, unmentionable thing can I possibly have done to you?

SUSAN: Married me?

RICK: Look, don't you think you two had better come inside. It's pouring with rain. Hadn't you noticed?

GERALD: Who cares, now? Who cares?

*(A slight pause. Just the sound of the rain.)*

*(Shrugging hopelessly)* Well . . .

*(From the house, MURIEL's voice is heard emitting a terrible wail.)*

*(Fearfully)* What, in the name of heaven, is that?

*(Another wail, slightly closer.)*

RICK: It's Auntie Muriel . . .

GERALD: Well, what does she—? Oh no, you haven't been setting fire to her as well, have you? Please tell me you haven't.

*(MURIEL comes staggering on, in her night attire and considerably distressed.)*

MURIEL: He's back . . . Gerald, he's back. Harry's come back to me . . .

RICK: Harry?

GERALD: It's all right. It's just her husband.

RICK: He's dead.

MURIEL: He's back. He's given me a sign, at last . . .

GERALD: Oh, dear heaven, what a dreadful night. Forgive us, oh Lord, for all we have done to offend thee. Forgive us . . .

MURIEL: Oh, Gerald, but it's such a terrible sign. Oh, Harry . . .

RICK: What's the problem, Auntie Muriel?

MURIEL: Rick, you'll have to come back in there with me. I can't go in there, not on my own . . . Not while he's there.

RICK: Auntie, I can't. Look at Mum, she's—

(MURIEL *lets out another wail.*)

GERALD: Go with her, Rick. It's nothing important. It happens to Muriel twice a week regularly. But for goodness' sake, go with her. Leave us. We'll manage somehow.

RICK: *(Starting to go)* Right. Are you sure? I won't be long . . .

MURIEL:   Come on, quickly, Ricky, quickly . . .

RICK:   Coming, Auntie. *(To his parents as he goes)* Don't get too wet, will you?

(RICK *and* MURIEL *go.* GERALD *and* SUSAN *continue to sit on the grass. The rain pours down.)*

GERALD:   *(Quietly)* Don't get too wet . . . Why did you do it, Susan? Do you hate me that much?

SUSAN:   I didn't do it. How many more times? But yes, as a matter of fact since you ask, I do hate you. Very much. But I didn't destroy your book, I promise. I think I know who did, though.

GERALD:   Who, if not you? Rick?

SUSAN:   No, not Ricky . . .

GERALD:   Well, who else is there? Muriel? A. J. P. Taylor, on a sudden jealous impulse? Who?

SUSAN:   Tony.

GERALD:   Tony? Tony who?

SUSAN:   My Tony. My brother Tony.

GERALD:   Don't be so absurd. You have no brother. You did it. You know you did, admit it.

SUSAN:   No, I didn't. Because I was out here. All the time. And Bill Windsor can vouch for that. He came back and was with me. Till he was thrown in the lake. So.

GERALD:   Lake? What lake? Bill came back, yes, and you then felt dizzy and we had to put you to bed. And there you stayed, in bed asleep, from 3 p.m. onwards, until you awoke in the small hours and embarked on your nocturnal maraudings.

SUSAN:   That's nonsense. I know what I was doing and it certainly wasn't that—

GERALD:   Oh, yes, it was. There are witnesses.

SUSAN:   *(Softly)* I'll never forget what I did. Ever.

(RICK *returns briefly with a dishcloth.*)

GERALD:   Well?

RICK:   Very peculiar.

GERALD:   What is?

RICK:   She was right. Someone's written on her bedroom ceiling . . .

GERALD:   On Muriel's ceiling?

RICK:   In chalk, it looks like. They must have climbed on her chest of drawers . . .

GERALD:   Oh, Susan . . . What was written? Don't tell me.

RICK:   It says, 'KNICKERS OFF, MURIEL.'

(SUSAN *laughs.*)

GERALD:    *(Deeply shocked)* Oh, Susan. How is Muriel taking it?

RICK:    She's OK. I told her to make us all a cup of cocoa. Take her mind off it . . .

GERALD:    *(Dully)* Cocoa?

RICK:    Won't be a minute. I'm going to clean it off for her.

*(RICK goes.)*

GERALD:    All that and now compulsory cocoa. Locusts follow shortly. *(Rising and extending a hand)* Susan, come on inside, please.

SUSAN:    *(Drawing back from him)* Go away, Gerald. Leave me alone.

GERALD:    Listen, I don't honestly have the energy left to drag you in by your hair. If you won't come of your own free will, then for your own sake, I shall be forced to phone an ambulance.

SUSAN:    Oh, not another ambulance . . .

GERALD:    You need to be looked after, Susan.

SUSAN:    I'm being looked after perfectly well, thank you. Now go away. *(Shouting)* Bugger off!

GERALD:    *(Defeated)* I'm going! I'm going! I give up, Susan, I give up. You've won. I'm afraid I can't do any more. That's it. Finished.

(GERALD *leaves.*)

SUSAN: *(After him, as he goes)* I don't care. I'm free of you all now, you see. All of you. You with your prim little, frigid little, narrow-minded little meanness. And that priggish brat who's ashamed of me. Who'd faint at the sight of a pair of tits. As for her with her dead husband. No wonder he died. *(Yelling)* What are you hoping for, Muriel? A phantom pregnancy? *(She laughs.)* Too late, dear. Too damn late. You and me both. Over the hill. Over the . . .

*(She suddenly feels sorry for herself. She becomes more plaintive and tearful. She looks around her.)*

*(In a small voice)* Where's everybody gone? They're all gone. *(Sings)* Rain, rain, go away . . . *(Calling softly)* Andy? *(She listens.)* Lucy? *(No reply.)* Tony? Remember me? *(Silence.)* Oh.

*(A clap of thunder.* TONY *appears in the distance. He carries an unopened umbrella. He seems quite unaffected by the rain.)*

TONY: *(Hailing her)* Susie!

SUSAN: Tony?

TONY: *(Approaching)* Dear Big Sis. What are you doing now? You'll catch your deather.

SUSAN: I know, I'm so silly. I got caught in the rain . . .

TONY: We really do have to keep an eye on you, don't we? You can't be trusted out on your own . . .

SUSAN: You'll just have to take care of me, Tony . . .

TONY:    *(Hugging her briefly)* We will. We will. *(Opening the umbrella)* Now, let's get you dry . . .

*(The umbrella when opened is seen to be more of a sunshade or even a parasol, intended for sun rather than rain.* TONY *holds it over* SUSAN'S *head. At once the weather is transformed. The rain stops. The sun shines and it is noon on a glorious country afternoon. The birds sing.)*

There! Isn't that better?

SUSAN:    Oh, yes. *(She looks around her with pleasure.)* Much, much better.

*(*TONY, *now we can see him more clearly, is wearing a smart country gentleman's suit with sporty waistcoat and a tweed cap. He seems dressed more for a day at the races than for a wedding. This impression is heightened by the steward's badge he is wearing on his lapel. Everything from here on is in a slightly heightened colour and design, suggesting* SUSAN'S *own extreme mental state. What we see are images remembered by her of films she has seen, books she has read, TV she has watched.)*

TONY:    Perfect day for it, isn't it?

SUSAN:    *(Happily)* Oh, yes. A perfect day for a wedding. Everything's perfect now . . .

*(*LUCY *comes rushing on excitedly. She is wearing a wedding dress but, as yet, no head dress. She carries a number of 'extras' for* SUSAN *who is still very much in her night-dress state. Simple things to effect a quick transformation. A hat, gloves, shoes and some dress trimmings.* LUCY *also helps* SUSAN *during the next.)*

LUCY: Oh, there you are, Mother. I wondered where you were . . .

SUSAN: Darling, you look beautiful—

LUCY: *(Kissing her lightly on the cheek)* Thank you. And you are quite hopeless. You know that, don't you?

SUSAN: *(With an amused glance to* TONY*)* Yes, darling . . .

LUCY: I thought that today you were all supposed to run round after me and not the other way round . . .

SUSAN: I'm sorry. I was dreadfully delayed. I had to supervise this new maid, Tess. Who's terribly slow and frightfully dim . . .

TONY: Don't worry. Lucy adores running round . . .

LUCY: No, I don't, shut up. Oh, Mummy, I'm terribly excited. I really am. I hope I'm going to be all right. That I won't let you and Daddy down.

SUSAN: You won't, darling. Don't worry. We'll both be here.

LUCY: *(Whispering)* You'll be there tonight if I need you, won't you?

SUSAN: I'll be there tonight if you need me, I promise.

*(*TONY *has sauntered off under this last.* SUSAN *is putting on her shoes. While she does so,* LUCY *surveys the scene.)*

LUCY: Isn't that main marquee just sensational? It must cover about three acres. And it's simply filled with flowers.

SUSAN: They're for you, darling. I got them all for you.

(ANDY *strolls on. He is wearing morning dress and a grey top hat. He has a pair of binoculars round his neck.*)

ANDY: Hallo, young Lucy.

LUCY: (*Running to kiss him*) Daddy, it's all perfect. Thank you. Thank you.

ANDY: We're doing our best. (*To* SUSAN) All right, darling?

SUSAN: Very happy. (*She mouths 'Thank you' to him.*)

(ANDY *throws a kiss to her in response.*)

ANDY: Incidentally, young lady, aren't you supposed to be ready for the off in a few minutes?

LUCY: (*Unconcernedly*) Plenty of time.

ANDY: Oh, yes? (*Producing a pocket watch and holding it up for her to see*)What does that say, then?

LUCY: Oh, gosh. Golly, is that really the time? Do excuse me, everyone. Sorry . . .

(LUCY *races off.* SUSAN *and* ANDY *watch her with affectionate amusement.*)

SUSAN: I've never seen her so excited. Thank you for making it so perfect for her, Andy. You're being terribly patient. You know what these things mean to us women.

ANDY:   If it makes you both happy, then I'm happy. I think everything's arrived anyway. Except the band. Where on earth has the band got to?

*(Exactly on cue a brass band strikes up in the distance with some cheerful tune.)*

That's more like it.

SUSAN:   Oh, they're rather jolly . . .

ANDY:   Are you sure? We've got a pipe band if you'd rather.

SUSAN:   No, these are fine.

*(*TONY *strolls back into view.)*

ANDY:   All OK, Tony?

TONY:   You bet. I've just been having a snoop round the brides' enclosure. Our Lucy looks as good as any of them, I must say . . .

SUSAN:   *(Rather puzzled)* Sorry?

ANDY:   Glad to hear it.

TONY:   I think she'll do it, you know. She's in peak condition, she's free of injuries and, of course, the going'll suit her.

ANDY:   She prefers it firm . . .

TONY:   Oh, yes.

SUSAN: What are you both talking about?

*(From the distance, over the band, the sound of the PA. It is hard to make out distinctly, but it seems to be announcing a list of runners for the next race.)*

ANDY: *(Hearing this)* Hallo. Things are getting started.

SUSAN: Will someone tell me what's going on?

TONY: Aha! Look who's here . . .

(BILL *enters. He is dressed in a rather loud, cliché bookie's suit. He still clutches his case as always. Only this one is emblazoned with the words* HONEST BILL.)

BILL: Afternoon, chaps.

SUSAN: *(Uncomprehendingly)* Bill?

BILL: Hallo, Susie.

ANDY: How's the betting been?

BILL: Oh, pretty brisk . . .

SUSAN: I thought this was a wedding.

ANDY: Put a tenner on for me, will you, Bill?

BILL: Will do. Each way?

SUSAN: Andy, I thought this was a wedding . . .

ANDY: *(Amused)* What's that about a wedding, you daft old

thing? *(Ignoring her again)* What are you offering, Bill? Ten to one?

TONY: You'll be lucky.

BILL: No way, five to four and that's generous. You won't get that anywhere else . . .

ANDY: What? She was thirty-three to one this morning . . .

BILL: No, that was the jockey. You can have thirty-three on him. Only five to four on the bride . . .

*(The three men laugh uproariously at this. SUSAN watches them incredulously.)*

SUSAN: Aren't they getting married?

BILL: Married? Who's getting married?

ANDY: Susie's got this thing about a wedding. She wants a wedding, for some reason . . .

TONY: Then you shall have a wedding, my darling . . .

SUSAN: I thought this was one . . .

BILL: Absolutely. Good things, weddings.

ANDY: *(His binoculars raised)* I think they're coming under orders . . .

SUSAN: *(Becoming increasingly concerned)* Andy? Andy?

ANDY: *(Absorbed)* Just a tick, darling . . .

BILL: *(Chattily, to* TONY) Glorious spot, this. Is it all yours?

TONY: Yes.

BILL: How long have you lived here?

TONY: Since 1386.

BILL: Oh, quite a time. Vast.

TONY: Yes, we go right to the river that way.

BILL: Oh, yes. I see. What's the other side, then?

TONY: Oh, that's Thailand . . .

BILL: Oh, is it? Is it?

TONY: We held on to the shooting rights, but it's theirs officially.

BILL: Lucky little chaps . . .

SUSAN: *(Becoming impatient with this talk)* Oh, really. Do be sensible.

BILL: And the lake there?

TONY: No, that's the Caspian Sea.

BILL: Is it? Is it? I always wondered where that was.

SUSAN: Look, will you stop it once, you two. You're spoiling it all.

ANDY:  *(Still with the glasses)* Ah! They're off . . .

BILL:  Splendid!

TONY:  Hoorah!

SUSAN:  Where's my wedding? What's happened to the wedding I was promised? I want a wedding . . .

ANDY:  Hold on, darling, hold on. There's a love. *(At the race)* Good girl . . . look at her go!

TONY:  Time for a glass of champers, I think, don't you?

BILL:  Rather.

TONY:  *(Yelling to someone in the far distance)* Champagne over here . . . Quick, quick . . .

ANDY:  She's lying third at the moment. But she's nicely positioned. Not letting herself get boxed in . . .

SUSAN:  *(Desperately to herself)* This isn't what I wanted at all. Not at all.

(MURIEL *comes across the lawn with a tray of champagne glasses. She is dressed in very formal maid's black bombazine, with cap and apron. Incongruously, she appears to be heavily pregnant.)*

MURIEL:  Here comes a lovely glass of champagne . . .

TONY:  Thank you, Muriel.

SUSAN:  *(Recognizing her)* Muriel?

MURIEL:  Just one moment, madam.

BILL:  *(Taking a glass of champagne)* Super. Just what the doc ordered.

*(TONY also helps himself. MURIEL does a lot of curtseying.)*

First rate band this. Who are they?

TONY:  Oh, they're all—hang on—who are they, Andy?

ANDY:  *(Still watching the race)* Odd job men . . .

TONY:  That's it. They're all odd job men. Cornish odd job men.

BILL:  Amazing.

MURIEL:  *(Offering susan a glass)* Madam?

SUSAN:  This is all getting so stupid . . .

ANDY:  She's going to win it, you know, she's going to win!

*(SUSAN reacts to something in her drink.)*

SUSAN:  Yeeurrk! This is disgusting. What's this in my drink?

MURIEL:  In the champagne, madam?

SUSAN:  It's disgusting, take it away.

MURIEL:  I think it's supposed to be there, madam. It was in the red tin.

TONY:   It's only a frog, Susie.

SUSAN:   A frog?

TONY:   If you don't like it, spit it out . . .

SUSAN:   *(Sharply)* Muriel, get out of that ridiculous uniform,
you look absurd . . .

MURIEL:   Yes, madam. *(Curtseying)* Thank you, madam.

TONY:   Get 'em off, Muriel.

(MURIEL *goes.*)

ANDY:   They've got about a furlong to go . . . It's Lucy
from Macramé Lad and Dead Hubby . . . and they're
well clear of Priggish Boy and Smug Vicar . . .

SUSAN:   *(Impatiently)* Andy . . .

ANDY:   Sorry, darling. Want a look?

SUSAN:   No, I don't. I've no desire to see our daughter pranc-
ing about singing dreadful songs in woolly animal ears.

ANDY:   Oh, come on, darling. It's only once a year. And it
means so much to the kid. *(Back to his binoculars)* And she's
there . . . she's nearly there . . . and she's done it! Lucy's done it!

TONY:   Well done, Lucy . . .

BILL:   *(With him)* Good for her. First rate. In my opinion as a doctor, your maid's pregnant again, Andy. I could be wrong, of course.

ANDY: 'Fraid she is, Bill. Every time there's a race meeting, same old story . . . Excuse me, I'm just going to congratulate Lucy . . . Terrific race. *(He starts to move off.)*

SUSAN: *(Vainly, after him)* Andy, wait . . .

*(At this moment, GERALD enters. He is dressed as an Archbishop.)*

ANDY: *(Greeting him like a long-lost brother)* Hey! Hey! Look who's better late than never. Gerry! By all that's holy!

GERALD: *(Embracing ANDY with equal fervour)* Andy, you old devil you . . .

SUSAN: *(Absolutely appalled)* Gerald?

TONY: Hallo, Gerry!

SUSAN: What's Gerald doing here?

GERALD: Tony, you old rascal . . . And there's Billy Beelzebub himself. Hallo, Bill.

BILL: Hallo, Gerry . . .

GERALD: Well, this is nice, isn't it? Isn't this nice?

SUSAN: Gerald, just go away. Go on, get away! Get away!

*(She is ignored. In fact, from this point on, people appear to be less and less aware of SUSAN. As if she herself were slowly slipping from the dream whilst it carries on without her.)*

ANDY: Where have you been, anyway?

GERALD: I do apologize, everyone. I had a divorce to perform. Last-minute job.

BILL: Oh, super. I love divorces.

ANDY: Now, you must come and meet Lucy . . .

(*But at this moment,* LUCY *comes rushing on breathlessly, her face flushed with excitement. She is dressed as before, but now wears her head dress. This is a standard bridal one, enlivened by the addition of a pair of built-in animal ears and a race winner's rosette. Behind her, she drags* RICK. *He is dressed as a sort of rickshaw driver—at least, as seen in various Hollywood oriental films.*)

LUCY: Daddy, we won. We won . . .

ANDY: I know, darling, I know . . .

SUSAN: (*Looking at the couple in horror*) No! Not him. Not him, Lucy darling, don't marry him . . . (*Shouting at* RICK) Go away, go away at once, Ricky! You're not to marry her, I forbid it.

LUCY: It's no good, Mother, he doesn't speak English.

TONY: They've been married for months, anyway.

ANDY: Never mind. I know you'll make Tess a fine husband, young man.

SUSAN: Tess?

RICK: *(In his normal voice)* I'll try, sir. I'll do my best to fatten her up and cut off her hair.

GERALD: God bless you, God bless you, God bless you . . .

*(At this point, everyone, with the exception of* SUSAN, *now totally ignored, gathers round the bride and groom and talks at once.* SUSAN *watches them with increasing fury.)*

LUCY: I knew I was going to win. I looked round during those final three furlongs and I could see the other two were getting weaker. And I felt as strong as ever. I could have run and run all day long. *(etc.)*

RICK: *(With her)* I knew we were in with a chance. But it was Tess, she was the one. She showed her convent training. I've never been so proud in my life. Don't worry, I'll take good care of her, you can be sure of that. *(etc.)*

ANDY: *(With them)* I had the glasses on you all the way. I was a bit concerned at the five furlong marker when you still hadn't made a break but I understood your tactics. I mean, the thing about having a fast finish is to use it, isn't it? *(etc.)*

TONY: *(With them)* I think the wonderful thing about racing is that it doesn't matter a damn about the races. The whole thing's one glorious social event, in my opinion, intended for the consumption of the maximum number of bottles of champers. *(etc.)*

BILL: *(With them)* This is the most glorious race course I've ever been on. I think it beats somewhere like Ascot into a top hat. I mean, you've got everything. Thailand over there and the Caspian. And the best of England as well. Magic. *(etc.)*

GERALD: *(With them)* You know, I haven't been here since—when would it be?—1386, I think. Can it be that long? You don't look a day older, Andy, old boy. I hope the same can be said about me. I doubt it. Some of us wear better than others, eh? *(etc.)*

SUSAN: *(After a moment of this)* This is grossly unfair, it really is. Why doesn't anyone take any notice of me? *(Louder)* Why won't you look at me? *(Very loudly)* LOOK AT ME AT ONCE, DO YOU HEAR? ALL OF YOU!!! *(She stamps her foot.)*

*(The band stops playing. Silence. Everyone turns to look at her. They seem slightly puzzled for a moment as to who she might be.)*

ANDY: *(Moving forward, as he remembers her)* Darling . . .

LUCY: Mother, how lovely . . .

*(They all surge forward to greet her. SUSAN is a little alarmed.)*

SUSAN: What are you all doing?

*(They surround her, greeting her as they do so. All seem pleased to see her. MURIEL comes on unobtrusively with more champagne. She is no longer pregnant.)*

RICK: *(Again, together with the others)* Hallo there, Mum. Good to see you . . .

GERALD: *(With him)* Hallo, Susan. Do you remember me? Gerald?

BILL: *(With them)* Hallo there. Are you still taking those pills I gave you?

TONY:   *(With them)* Hallo, Big Sis. Where have you been hiding away?

ANDY:   *(Over this)* Ladies and Gentlemen . . . I have . . . Ladies and Gentlemen . . .

*(The chatter dies down.)*

*(Seeing)* Have we got some fresh champagne there, Muriel? Splendid. Pass it round.

MURIEL:   Yes, sir. *(Confidentially, with a furtive look in* SUSAN's *direction)* The ambulance is on its way . . .

ALL:   *(Except* SUSAN, *furtively to* MURIEL) Shhh!

*(There is a single clap of thunder. One or two react but the weather remains unalterably sunny.* MURIEL *passes amongst them. Those with no glasses take one. Those with empty ones take full ones.* SUSAN *is not offered one and seems, during the course of things, to have lost her original glass.)*

ANDY:   *(As* MURIEL *performs her duties)* You've had the baby all right, I see, Muriel?

MURIEL:   Yes, sir. Thank you, sir.

ANDY:   What was it? Another boy?

MURIEL:   Yes, sir.

ANDY:   And what are you going to call him? Let me guess?

MURIEL:   Harry, sir.

ANDY:   Splendid. That'll be—how many—now?

MURIEL:   This'll be my tenth Harry, sir.

ANDY:   Well done. Keep going.

*(A small ripple of applause.* MURIEL *looks embarrassed.)*

*(Seeing they are all set)* Now then. Muriel, grab yourself a glass, you must join us for this—

(MURIEL *does so, standing just a little apart from the circle.*

Ladies and Gentlemen, I want to propose a toast to the woman who is not simply the most important person in my life—but I suspect, is the most important person in all our lives . . .

ALL:   *(Variously)* Hear . . . hear . . . absolutely . . . *(etc.)*

ANDY:   Susan, you are uniquely precious to us all. You are irreplaceable.

(SUSAN *glows.)*

So, without further frills. To you, dearest Susie.

ALL:   *(Toasting)* Dearest Susie.

*(They drink.)*

TONY:   Speech . . .

LUCY:   Yes, speech, Mummy . . .

SUSAN: *(Deferentially)* No, no . . .

ALL: *(Variously)* Yes, yes . . . speech . . . come on, Susie, speech . . .

(SUSAN, *still standing amongst them, smiles in acceptance. She bows her head slightly in thought and then starts her speech. The others step back so that she stands in a larger circle than before.*)

SUSAN: Dearest friends. Family. My happiest moment has been to stand here with you all and share this, my most precious of days. I grow hugh, summer few bald teddy know these two wonderful children, Lucy and Rick. I cannot tell you how heaply cowed siam.

*(As she continues to speak the lights begin to fade round her until finally she is isolated.)*

Tinny beers a show. High december how rotten high trade fat haywood throw twig and throng hike hair share rents. Pie lank hod hat day lid! Hens, hang few saw paw up-short. Hang few. Hang few, hens, sizzle pie tart insole. Grey ice way chew . . . ? *(She hesitates.)* Grey ice way—?

*(She is aware that people seem to be getting harder to see. She is starting to be lit now by the reflection of an ambulance's blue flashing light.)*

Hair growing, hens? Goosey? Gandy? Chair old? *(Pause.)* Hair shone? Hair hall shone? Tone show, fleas. Fleas, tone show. December bee? Choose 'un. December choosey. December bee? December bee?

*(The others have frozen in the shadows. They appear neither to see nor to hear her now.*

SUSAN *gives a last despairing wail. As she does so, the lights fade to blackout.)*